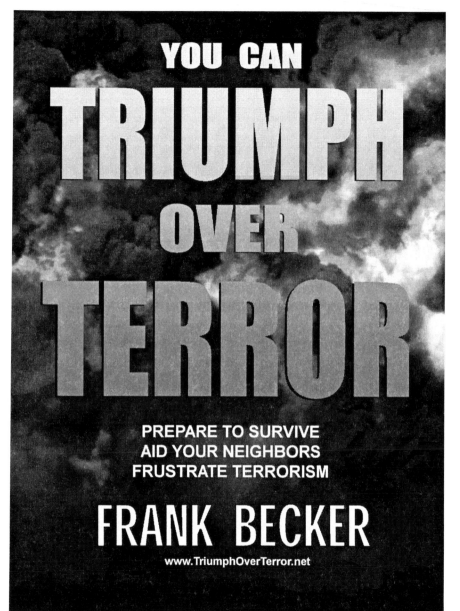

YOU CAN
TRIUMPH
OVER
TERROR

PREPARE TO SURVIVE
AID YOUR NEIGHBORS
FRUSTRATE TERRORISM

FRANK BECKER

www.TriumphOverTerror.net

Text, photographs, and drawings ©copyright 2005 by Frank Becker.

Published 2005 by Greenbush Press, 21518 Karpathos Ln, Spring, TX 77388. Greenbush and the Greenbush Publishing logo are trademarks of Greenbush Press.

Printed by Fidlar-Doubleday in the United States of America.

Library of Congress Catologing-in-Publication Data is on file with the publisher.

ISBN 0-9766720-0-6

ISBN 0-9766720-0-6

9 780976 672005   52495

To Joy!

Acknowledgements

I will be forever grateful to my wife Joy—teacher, writer, speaker, radio commentator, partner, pal and mother—for the years of love, encouragement and hard work that helped bring this and other projects to fruition. I also want to thank each of our wonderful children and their families—Sandy and Joe, Cheryl and Michael, Jamie and Jenn, who made significant contributions to this book, and Matt and Daniela.

My late father, John S. Becker, and my mother, Loretta Becker Hull, provided a unique opportunity for us children to learn diverse trades and crafts, and were unstinting in underwriting the cost of the first fallout shelter.

My three brothers deserve special mention. John and Bill undertook the lion's share of construction and produced many innovative features for that first 1962 sub-surface shelter. John reviewed the chapters dealing with shelter design and engineering for this book. Bob—formerly Vice-President of Advertising at Eckerd Drugs and one of Jack Eckerd's inner circle during the early days—created the original cover design.

It's impossible to recognize all of the people who have, encouraged us through the years. Foremost among them are included Al and Helen Salay, trusted counselors and confidantes, along with John Sipos, broadcast journalist, and his wife Diane, all very close friends of four decades, as well as the late William F. Adams, Jr., a childhood friend who stuck closer than a brother through nearly six decades of friendship, with his sister Linda and with his wife Mary.

Others who have encouraged me include Henry and Lois Flora, Walter and Dawn Bates, Bill and Linda Womer, John and Carol Kenzy, Bill and May McMahon, Paul and Pauline Morrissette, Joe and Donna Flynn, Stan and Heather Birnbaum, Kevin and Gertrude Nicholas, John and Susan Bassani, Linda Bennett, Judie Regitano, Almon Bartholomew, and too many others to include here.

May God bless their lives and works!

Contents

Foreword

Earth. It looks serene in those NASA pictures taken from space. It is not serene.

In every generation, Earth is a place of cataclysm and catastrophe. Some of the dangers come from space in the form of radiation or asteroids. Some come from the Earth below in the form of volcanos or earthquakes. The atmosphere itself contributes tornados and hurricanes and massive snow storms In ages past, we would have added wild animals and famine to the list. Today we add strange new diseases, poisons and atomic radiation. Some are even created and dispersed by men for their own evil purposes. No! Earth is not serene. People have responded in various ways to these many threats.

Some have found the very thought of these possibilities beyond their ability to endure. To contemplate them would be to succumb to panic. They have closed the doors of their minds and gone on with life as if there were no threats at all.

Some have focused closely and have become desperate, deciding to live it up while they can because the whole matter is hopeless. Disaster and death are nigh.

Some are oblivious.

Some, a very few, have made a rational evaluation. They have recognized what cannot be done and what can be done. They have decided that what can be done must be done. They have decided that they are responsible for their own welfare and that of their families. They have realized that government cannot do it all. Then they have proceeded to discern and do that which can be done. They have even volunteered to help others to find their way down that same path, "The Path of What Can Be Done."

Frank Becker, in creating this manual of preparation, has provided just such help. He speaks from a vantage point gained over a lifetime. He has observed the same terrors many others of his generation have observed, but perhaps with a slightly different perspective. He has admitted the horror but, rather than yielding to it, he has studied the means by which we may triumph over it.

To those who want to know about the path to triumph, this book, "You Can Triumph Over Terror," will be a wonderful resource. It will be a treasure. Yes, this is a fearsome topic. To be able to discuss it without wrapping it up in passion and fear is remarkable - but necessary. Passion and fear can immobilize. Triumph takes action. Frank Becker has given us that necessary view. Action is the antidote for fear.

—Alexander W. Salay
March 2, 2005

Introduction

This book takes an "upbeat approach" to a downbeat subject. We can't put a good spin on terrorism or a natural disaster. A positive mental outlook won't by itself be sufficient to change the course of history. But you and I can make a difference in this world.

If you are willing to invest a little time and a few bucks, you will accomplish four things. You will significantly improve your chances of survival, you will lift a burden from government, you may position yourself to help others, and you will help frustrate the terrorists who are hellbent on destroying your way of life.

Don't let terror terrify you! Instead, take positive steps to stymie the efforts of the terrorists.

"A MATTER OF TIME"

As an American, you should prepare yourself for the perils that threaten you. You already know that natural disasters, such as hurricanes, earthquakes, ice storms and tornadoes, are a regular occurrence. You should also realize that major terrorist attacks are only "a matter of time."

THE HOUSTON CHRONICLE
February 16, 2005

Al-Queda remains determined to carry out its terror campaign, and the brutality of attacks will escalate, a United Nations team that's monitoring sanctions against the group said in a report Tuesday. Al-Queda still has a strong interest in acquiring chemical, biological, radiological and nuclear weapons and it's only 'a matter of time' before an attack, the report says.

"The biggest fear we all have is terrorists getting hold of the means to cause a mass attack," said Richard Barrett, the team's coordinator. "Al-Queda is a phenomenon that observes no borders. It is even harder to track now than it was a year or two ago, when it had a more coherent structure and leadership," he said.

THE WASHINGTON TIMES
February 17, 2005

Senior U.S. intelligence leaders told Congress yesterday that "it may only be a matter of time" before terrorists try to use weapons of mass destruction against the United States.

In his first public appearance since becoming CIA director in September, Porter J. Goss used the annual worldwide threat hearing to issue the prediction, while another federal official said the FBI knows little about al-Qaeda sleeper cells such as the September 11 terrorists.

"It may be only a matter of time before al-Qaeda or another group attempts to use chemical, biological, radiological and nuclear weapons," Mr. Goss told the Senate Select Committee on Intelligence.

TIME IS NOT ON YOUR SIDE

When the new CIA director said, "...only a matter of time," he could not say how much time. An attack could be weeks or even days away.

You need to plan and prepare for terrorist attacks now. Today! The sooner you begin, the better your chances of survival.

Don't look to the politicians to try to shock you into preparing. They have already provided substantial resources through FEMA for anyone who is interested, but they are not going to risk losing the next election by frightening voters to the point that they ju into the camp of their political opponents.

PREPARATION WILL YIELD BENEFITS

By planning and preparing, you will achieve the following:

1. You will improve your own chances of surviving the emergency.

2. You will be equipped for the period of confusion and for the shortages of food and water that inevitably follow a major disaster.

3. You will lift a burden from the shoulders of FEMA and your local emergency organizations because, unlike others, you may not require immediate assistance. The people and precious materials that might have been required by you can be devoted to meeting the needs of others, as well as pursuing, combatting and apprehending any criminal perpetrators.

4. You will be in a position to help others less fortunate than you, neighbors who may have lost their homes or have been injured in the course of the attack.

5. You will make the terrorist's work a lot harder for them.

When you join millions of other people in preparing, you all become much less vulnerable to attack. You collectively frustrate the terrorists. You negate their efforts. You help defeat them!

When you prepare for terror and other emergencies, you become part of the solution, rather than part of the problem. You become an American hero.

Most of us take precautions against dangers that threaten us or our property. We make simple preparations.

We fear fire, but we do not let that fear rule our lives. We do, however, take measures to protect ourselves. We install smoke detectors to warn us of fire. We buy fire extinguishers to fight those fires. We take these precautions because they are mandated by law or our insurance companies, but also because we sincerely want to limit damage to our property, to save lives, and to be in a position to recover economically. These are prudent measures.

When someone installs a sprinkler system in a home or a business, they aren't simply preparing to extinguish a fire. They are also inhibiting the action of arsonists. When a criminal sees that you have prepared to frustrate his efforts—whether by installing sprinkler systems, closed-circuit surveillance systems, detection devices, alarms, or guards—he also realizes that his efforts to exploit you may very well fail. And he may go to jail. So he walks down the street, looking for an easier target.

When we prepare ourselves for emergencies, we are actually fighting back, pushing away the evil from us. Terrorists who plan to harm us are inevitably discouraged when we take precautions to stop them.

That's the key. Prepare for emergencies. Then get on with your life.

When enough Americans look at the dangers of terrorism the same way that they look at the risk of a house fire or an automobile accident, we will all be a lot better off.

One hundred years ago, society was basically agrarian. Many people lived on farms. Even urban dwellers understood that harvests came in at certain times of the year. Each fall most people had to process and store the food that they would require for the following year. They couldn't go to a super market and buy a frozen pizza or a TV dinner. They knew that if they didn't have enough food set aside, they would go hungry or starve.

But when an emergency disrupts the supply of fuel, food, and electricity, we all wish that we had kept more food, bottled water and flashlight batteries on hand.

The purpose of terrorism is to destabilize economies, shatter societies, and bring down governments so that society is left defenseless and prey to the terrorist's perverted ideas about how the world should be run.

The media likes to keep us uneasy, insecure, and worried, continually glued to our TV screens. News departments want high ratings and the revenue associated with them. Politicians want our votes and the power associated with them. Many want to keep us continually on edge and even in fear. And, oddly enough, that's precisely what the terrorists want us to feel.

In the 1952 motion picture, "Deadline, USA," a writer is asked, "What's the difference between a journalist and a reporter?" He replies, "A journalist makes himself a part of the story; a reporter is only a witness." Not much has changed in 50 years. Now we have controversies over the roles of journalists. Some, like Dan Rather, are accused of trying to manipulate public opinion, while very few simply report the news and let you decide.

Destabilizing a culture is one of the first steps in the process of destroying it. Hitler continually propagandized that the German people had enemies within and enemies without. He vilified the Jewish people as the enemy within, and characterized any nation that did not bow to his insane ambitions as an enemy without. Playing upon the fears of the German people, he polarized society and was thus able to wrest their liberties away, replacing them with his demonic socialist dictatorship.

God grant that America never becomes so paralyzed by fear that we trade our constitutionally guaranteed liberties for some specious promise of peace. Beware those demagogues who attempt to create racial, religious, ethnic, or class strife for their own political advantage.

If Americans prepare themselves for natural emergencies and terrorist attacks, they will not be subject to such scare tactics. They will not be as insecure and uneasy about the reports they hear. Members of the media and political demagogues will not so easily manipulate their thinking. And the terrorists will be able to inflict far less damage, while paying a much higher price for each successive attack.

As we encourage the spread of democracy, and offer meaningful assistance to freedom loving peoples, we will also discourage tyrannical governments. They will have difficulty keeping their own people under an iron heal. And it will become increasingly difficult for terrorists to recruit suicidal fanatics from among dwindling ranks of zealots. Terrorists will have fewer holes to crawl into, their numbers will decline, and freedom loving people will find it increasingly easy to isolate and capture or kill them.

We are not to be terrified of the terror that comes by darkness. Of course we don't want to die in a terrorist attack. But we also don't want to live in a constant state of fear. So we need to invest in the anti-terror equivalent of a home fire extinguisher and stop allowing the news "commentators" and unscrupulous politicians from igniting fear in our hearts. We each need to invest a few bucks and a few hours to prepare ourselves.

The English were able to persevere in the face of Hitler's relentless bombing of London during World War II because they set their minds and hearts on the job to be done. They made their preparations and dug in until we Americans finally joined them and together, by God's grace, we were able to turn the tide.

You will actually help defeat terrorism by preparing to defend yourself. You will become part of a voluntary informal network as you keep your eyes peeled for suspicious activities.

But you must keep on with business as usual. You need to take your vacations, to travel, to laugh and play, to live and love. Of prime importance, try to love your enemies and do good to those who despitefully use you. President Bush demonstrated that spirit when he spearheaded the distribution of massive aid to the victims of the southeast Asian tsunami in December, 2004.

No man is an island. In a sense, we are our brother's keepers, and we should always keep in mind that we must help others as we would want to be helped. As Jesus said, "No greater love has any man than this, that he lays down his life for another." His teaching is the antithesis of that of the terrorists who lay down their lives to destroy others.

This is not to preach selfless self-sacrifice, but to argue that we should be keeping other people in mind even as we prepare to protect ourselves from terrorism.

Jesus said, "Do unto others as you would that they should do unto you." Stop them. Punish them if necessary. But forgive them. Demonstrate the right way by example. Perhaps their peers, who have not wholly entered into this madness, will be persuaded that peace and freedom are superior to brutal dictatorships. Help them also to become part of the solution rather than part of the problem.

Above all, you must avoid a bunker mentality. You do not have to become a survivalist in order to survive. But you must make reasonable preparations.

I have heard a self-serving preacher discourage his flock from taking steps to protect themselves. He boasted that God will provide his needs and those of his parishioners, so they needn't divert any funds from the support of the church. As a pastor, I encouraged my congregation to take reasonable steps to prepare for emergencies. Why should we tempt God? The Lord gave us ample guidance through the Old Testament account of Joseph, who stored grain during the seven good years so that there would be sufficient food to save the nation during the prophesied seven bad years. Let us not become a burden on others. Out of our prosperity, we Americans made generous offerings to the victims of the Asian tsunami. Can we now be prudent enough to set aside something so that we will have sufficient food in a time of need. Will we prove ourselves as generous as the Christians of ancient Macedonian who, out of their severe trial and extreme poverty, came to the assistance of others (II Cor 8).

We are engaged in a worldwide war against terrorism. All you need to do is make simple preparations that will cost a few bucks and requires very little time. Once you have completed these preparations, you will attain a meaningful sense of peace and can return wholeheartedly to this business of living.

Your preparation, combined with those of millions of other Americans, will lift an enormous burden from our federal and state governments and make it much more difficult for a terror attack to be effective beyond the initial effective range of any weapon that they are able to bring to bear.

Disclaimer

The information and opinions expressed in this book are offered to assist readers in protecting and preserving lives during an emergency, particularly a terrorist attack. They are offered in hopes that they will help you survive what might otherwise be a hopeless situation.

The kinds of attacks that might occur and the weapons that might be employed are only a matter of conjecture. An attack made with a weapon of mass destruction could kill hundreds of thousands of people, with many times that suffering injury.

This book provides information to help you survive varied emergencies and to assist you in minimizing damage. Much of this information has been gleaned from the websites of the American Red Cross and FEMA, as well as numerous books and articles, plus forty years of personal experience and study.

The suggestions offered, as well as the designs shown and the lists of items provided, may prove valuable in saving and sustaining lives.

If, however, someone builds a fallout shelter, and a conventional nuclear weapon is later detonated within a few hundred yards, that fallout shelter will be of little or no value. Everything within a radius of a quarter mile will probably be vaporized in a nanosecond. And if you put on a surgical face mask at the first sign of a biological weapon attack, but fail to cover any open wounds on your body, you are still apt to become infected.

The author cannot, of course, predict the occurrence, location, scope or severity of any natural disaster or act of war, and certainly cannot and will not take responsibility for the diverse application of the ideas contained within this book across an infinite variety of possible emergency and attack scenarios.

Every reader is encouraged to study this subject thoroughly, not relying simply upon this book, but reviewing materials produced by FEMA, The American Red Cross, and other experts on WMDs, implementing any suggestions prayerfully, while trusting God for his blessings on your efforts.

STEP ONE,

Ponder the Possibilities

1. Terror's Threat

YOUR TICKET IN THE TERROR LOTTERY

Without your knowledge or permission, you have been entered in a sort of reverse lottery, a lottery in which no one wants his name drawn, a lottery in which anyone who draws a winning number is automatically a loser.

The prize winners in this lottery are determined not by the arbitrary selection of little balls with numbers painted upon them, but by the deranged and fanatical minds of terrorists. They decide in what unexpected place, at what indeterminable time, and among what unsuspecting victims they will detonate their next bomb or release their latest toxin. The person whose name is drawn, whose number comes up, whose time has arrived, may suffer sickness, injury, and very possibly, death.

The purpose of this evil exercise is to terrorize and cow entire nations. The frequent result of their combined bullying is that nations bows down and appeases the perpetrators.

This tactic recently succeeded in Spain changing the result of the presidential election. Similar bullying, blackmail, and bribery has succeeded in many other countries, as well as in the halls of the United Nations.

Once again we are being painfully exposed to the reality that those who refuse to learn from history are doomed to repeat it.

The problem is that appeasement doesn't work. It simply opens the door to additional bullying. It encourages reigns of terror by the likes of Adolph Hitler, Joseph Stalin, and Saddam Hussein. Again and again, we learn that all that is necessary for evil to triumph is that good men do nothing.

Once again we are being painfully exposed to the reality that those who refuse to learn from history are doomed to repeat it.

3 OUT OF 4 AMERICANS EXPECT ANOTHER MAJOR ATTACK

On November 3rd, 2004, there was a collective sigh of relief from millions of Americans. They had feared that the wrong man in the White House would dramatically increase the odds of a successful terrorist attack upon the United States. Others believed that we are now in even greater danger because of the result of the election.

Yet, on that same election day, pollsters determined that 76% of all Americans expect another major terrorist attack.

Unfortunately, in spite of the outcome of the election, most Americans continue to rely upon government to prevent terror attacks and keep them safe.

We Americans have good reason for our apprehension. We are joined in our anxiety by our elected leaders, intelligence experts, law enforcement officers, emergency management personnel, the military, and spokesmen for both political parties. Virtually all knowledgeable authorities believe that an attack that is much deadlier than that of 9/11 is inevitable.

This book is not a survival manual. "Survivalists" are often perceived as gun-toting, wilderness-dwelling, antisocial fanatics. This book is written for the majority of Americans who are responsible, hard-working, peace-loving, God-fearing individuals. It is written for those of you who want to know how to prepare yourselves so that you can survive and help preserve our way of life. This book recommends steps that you may take to prepare yourself for both natural and man made disasters.

There are two kinds of terrorism. The first is the mom and pop home-grown variety which is organized on a small scale, but can still do enormous damage. The Oklahoma City bombing is an example. The other is organized across national borders, well-funded, and broad based. Through the use of terror and political blackmail, it is meant to bring down civilization and replace it with a corrupt quasi-religious government that is archaic, destructive, and devoid of individual liberties.

Even some American defeatists seem to champion this evil cause. They have spouted a pseudo-intellectual policy of appeasement. They would submit our sovereign nation to the control of socialist internationalists to gain the accolades of corrupt nations. Such people are not fit to govern because they have already violated the oath that they will uphold and protect the Constitution of the United States.

BLACKMAILING OF GOVERNMENTS

And they are sowing the dragon's teeth of destruction. For out of their influence will spring up an evil harvest like that which arose after British Prime Minister Neville Chamberlain joined the French in pleading futilely with the Nazis for "peace in our time." That weak-kneed appeasement resulted in World War II. And the aftermath still poisons our world.

The Spanish have attempted to appease these terrorists, hoping that they will go away and leave them alone. They have not done so. It's like trying to appease the bully in the schoolyard. Such a simpering show of weakness simply encourages bullies to believe that they can take over the entire world through intimidation, bribery and murder.

Hussein made fools of the so-called statesmen in the United Nations and across Europe and Asia by successfully bribing top leaders to allow him to pervert the Oil for Food program. If the terrorists are not stopped, they will gain control of one nation at a time, starting with the weakest first, building terrorist bases and training camps in each conquered country, killing off all opposition, increasing the scope and effectiveness of their threat as they pick off one enemy at a time until the have surrounded and isolated their ultimate enemy. That may sound extreme, but we are dealing with extremists. That's why they are fighting so hard to keep Iraq from becoming a democracy. When the United States won wars in Afghanistan and Iraq, it effectively closed scores of the terrorist's premier training camps.

Terrorism is a self-perpetuating horror, based on suspicion, hatred, fear, and the "eye for an eye and a tooth for a tooth" doctrine. It is promoted by people who still live in largely feudalistic and totalitarian societies. Close neighbors distrust and hate one another and they are frequently involved in tribal warfare.

The god of terrorism is satan, the evil one, Beelzebub, the devil, who is understood in most cultures to be the epitome of evil. His goal is to set brother against brother, father against son, and nation against nation. Jesus said that he is come to divide and destroy and conquer. His brings pestilence and famine and death and all of the other horrors associated with war.

TERRORISM ATTEMPTS TO TERRIFY

President Franklin Roosevelt put it well: "The only thing that we have to fear is fear itself." For fear is the currency of the terrorist movement. Terrorism's goal is to terrify its adversaries.

To Terrify You

When you see the heinous acts of terrorists splashed across your TV screen, you are apt to become stressed and traumatized. Some would have you try to treat the symptoms of this problem. The correct mindset is to prepare to destroy the enemy and thus remove the cause of the trauma.

To Terrify Your Children

I recall having to learn to "duck and cover," that little exercise where, at the sound of a siren, we third graders would crawl under our desks en masse and wait for the half-feared, half-hoped for explosion that would signal new excitement in our lives. We weren't really frightened because our world was very small and our understanding very limited.

When a child hears that someone has been killed by terrorists in a distant country whose name they can barely pronounce, they may feel regret, but they will not consider it a matter for personal anxiety. The media loves to make much of the trauma that children suffer, but children are probably the most resilient of us all. But their understanding will increase if a disaster or terrorist attack comes close enough to make it a matter of personal danger. Then you will be very glad that you've prepared.

To Terrify Your Family & Friends

During the Cuban Missile Crisis, I inspired the construction of a large family fallout shelter. It was an impressive undertaking, one which my father enthusiastically financed and to which my two older brothers contributed vital ideas, ingenious designs and hard labor.

President Kennedy had announced to the entire nation on television that the Soviet Union had established missiles on Cuban soil that would be capable of reaching much of the continental United States. Although our government was later able to defuse the missile crisis, and we were verbally assured that the Soviet Union had removed the missiles from Cuba, few believed the claim. The Cubans and Soviets never allowed us to conduct on-site inspections. Photographs taken from our reconnaissance aircraft high overhead revealed large wooden crates on the decks of cargo ships leaving Cuba, and we were told that these contained all of the nuclear-tipped missiles. Few Americans believed it.

With the very real possibility that missiles with nuclear warheads were hidden in hardened silos just ninety miles off the Florida Coast, a veritable flurry of shelter construction continued. Most of this construction was done with as much secrecy as possible because people feared that, in the event of an attack, those who had failed to prepare would mob those who had in order to gain shelter.

Not everyone was enthused with our efforts to survive a nuclear holocaust. One woman was adamant in her declaration that she would neither be involved in our plans nor, under any circumstances, set foot in our shelter. In fact, the only reason her husband was allowed to work on the shelter was because he was on my father's payroll. She declared that she would not live in a world spoiled by nuclear war. What's more, it was clear that she would not allow either her husband or her child this opportunity for survival.

In contrast, a man who resided in my father's manufactured housing residential development, a veteran of World War II, warned me that in the event of a nuclear attack, he would kill me an my entire family in order to take our shelter away from us. He would relent only if my father constructed a shelter large enough to house the entire population of the development, about 200 people.

Such were the passions aroused during those trying times. Such were two radically different views on the value of a fallout shelter. One person said, "I wouldn't be caught dead in one." Another warned, "I'll kill you in order to get yours." Clearly, terror affects different people differently.

To Terrify Society In General

The entire purpose of terrorism is to terrorize. Terrorism's goal is to destabilize societies so that the terrorists can take control of entire nations, one after another.

A Cloud of Fear

We've lived under the threat of total nuclear war since shortly after World War II when we learned that Soviet spies had stolen the secrets of the atomic bomb and that the Russians had successfully built and tested one. Early on, those of us in the public schools underwent frequent air raid drills.

The adults feared for our tender psyches, and we grew up in an environment of fear. Perhaps that constant state of fear helped kindle the sexual revolution as well as the drug and anti-war cultures.

Our post World War II parents may not have been very realistic. After all, they based their entire system of discipline on Dr. Spock's advice. Still, most little boys grow up with a sense of fearless adventure and a comforting confidence that they will survive as heroes, not die as cowards. Such is the bravado of the young, that they'd rather die for the right than live in slavery to evil.

After the Soviets stole the secrets for the infinitely more powerful hydrogen bomb, conditions again changed. The air raid sirens still sat atop tall buildings, but our leaders decided, without telling us, that they would no longer sound them in a major city like New York or Chicago. "Why panic the populace?" they reasoned. With these Intercontinental Ballistic Missiles traveling at 25,000 miles per hour, it would be impossible to evacuate 8-million New Yorkers during those 15 fateful minutes before the 5-megaton warheads struck ground zero. Never mind that people might have belatedly used their few remaining minutes to try to make peace with God.

There was a strong pro-communist sentiment in the United States. Much disinformation was peddled, lies were repeated, and confusion and fear were spread. (Much as it is now being spread.) As a result, so many people became fatalists that it was impossible to motivate the congress and executive branch to undertake a massive civil defense effort. The left promulgated the phrase, "Better Red than dead," and many Americans, not recognizing the living death that communism represents, echoed it.

So, appeasement reigned, just as it threatens to do again today. The doctrine of "mutually assured destruction" (MAD) was born. If the Russians attacked us, we would plaster them. And visa versa. Nobody would win. Everybody would lose. So, hopefully, nobody would attack anybody. Of course, if there were a madman at the controls, no amount of assured mutual destruction or appeasement would matter. Hundreds of millions would die.

Since our government failed to help its citizens prepare for the worst, many citizens decided to take on that responsibility themselves. Even among the impoverished, many with insight and imagination decided to relocate to rural and mountainous areas where they perceived the bombs were not likely to fall.

It was not until President Reagan called the U.S.S.R. an "Evil Empire," and demanded, "Mr. Gorbachev, tear down this wall!" that we discovered a national will and achieved victory in the cold war. It was not appeasement, but strength with honor, that ended the cold war.

Governmental agencies are currently concentrating on the prevention of mass murder and destruction, such as the crashing of planes into tall buildings and the use of WMDs. But terrorists constantly search for vulnerabilities. They look for places where their attacks will do grave damage and allow them to escape unscathed. A fanatic with a small bomb or a firearm can simply walk into a crowded waiting room and take a number of lives. Suicide bombings are only useful to them where they have sufficient fanatical recruits to carry them out over an extended period.

When a country is beset with constant attacks, such as in Iraq and Israel, the citizens begin to realize that, "It could happen to me."

If we prepare for terror, we will effectively reduce its potential to harm us. We will discourage it. But if we allow ourselves to be terrorized, the terrorists will have succeeded in crippling our national will. They will have won.

2. Terror's Weapons

Terror's primary weapon is fear. Terrorists employ unspeakable methods to kill or corrupt their enemies. At the same time, they attack the innocent, in order to destabilize societies, wreck economies and overturn governments.

They use whatever weapons they can get their hands on, and practice every heinous act, including suicide bombings, arson, kidnapping, torture, murder, and even the beheading of live victims.

If and when they are able to get their hands on weapons of mass destruction—nuclear, biological, radiological and chemical, they will feel justified in using them.

SUICIDE BOMBINGS, KIDNAPPING & ASSASSINATION

Favorite terrorist methods include bombings, kidnappings and assassinations. But even in the event of major attacks, like 9/11, a majority of people can be saved if they have been mentally prepared and properly equipped. This preparation requires very little effort or expense.

The 9/11 airline attacks on New York's Twin Towers were successful because they generated an intensely hot fire that weakened posts and beams and resulted in the buildings collapsing. Yes, the impact and attendant explosion and fire would have killed most of the people on one or two floors, but if it had not been for the thousands of gallons of jet fuel continuing to burn, the buildings would not have collapsed. Deaths would have been in the hundreds, not thousands, toxic chemicals and dangerous particulates would not have been spread for miles around, and economic loss would have been limited.

Many of the people who died in the attack might have escaped if they had attempted to do so early on. Fire and smoke were one of the great dangers they had to contend with, and they often are a danger in terrorist attacks.

The simple little 5 ounce "Pocket Pack" described in Chapter 8 contains inexpensive items to improve your chances to escape a fire.

Up until now, terrorists have used explosives for most of their attacks world wide, though they very successfully used hijacked airliners as flying bombs on 9-11. Although Saddam Hussein used WMDs against his own people, the Bush administration has thus far been able to prevent his minions from launching such an attack upon the United States.

The phrase, "weapons of mass destruction" (WMD), includes different kinds of weapons, but each can potentially kill millions of people in one strike. Nuclear weapons may generate massive explosions, but their greatest danger is the spread of radioactive particles over vast areas. Biological contagions are often spread by their victims. They probably represent the greatest threat to our civilian population. Chemical toxins produce horrible illness or death to those they contact.

Sometimes it is best to flee from these, weapons, while at other times it's best to remain where you are and to isolate yourself from them.

NUCLEAR WEAPONS

These weapons are of greatest threat to the "masses," to you and to me. Yes, conventional nuclear weapons will destroy entire cities, including structures and people, and can turn a once thriving metropolis into a poisoned ruin. The weapons that terrorists are more likely to use, however, may decimate the population while leaving the buildings standing. These are the biological, chemical and small and very dirty nuclear weapons that will kill or incapacitate thousands of people in one attack.

Radiation—Powerful, Pervasive, and Deadly

Perhaps the WMD that is most difficult and costly to protect against is the nuclear weapon because of the powerful, pervasive, and deadly radiation emitted.

Nuclear radiation is emitted by particles of material that are made radioactive when a nuclear weapon is detonated. Hundreds of thousands of tons of concrete and steel may be turned into radioactive dust that will be blown into the atmosphere by such an explosion, then carried around the world by stratospheric winds. As these particles fall from the atmosphere, the radiation they emit travels in a straight line to penetrate the roofs, windows and walls of buildings. Any people or animals who are out of doors in the vicinity of the bomb's detonation will be radiated. It is absorbed into the root systems of plants and travels into the food chain where it is ingested by human beings and remains in their vital organs to cause leukemia and other deadly diseases. Even the contents of metal cans, such as vegetables or fruits, can be made radioactive. Human beings who are heavily exposed will suffer severe damage to their connective tissue and internal organs.

Nuclear radiation cannot be seen, tasted, or smelled. It is a silent killer. It destroys your immune system, damages your body cells and bone marrow, and makes you prone to cancer. If you are standing outside within a couple of miles of a nuclear detonation, it may burn your skin off, or even vaporize you.

The radiation dosage can be weak, if you are a long way from its source, or strong, if you are nearby. A short exposure to an intense dosage is not very different from a long exposure to a low dosage. The effect is cumulative. That's why the dental X-ray attendants drape a lead apron around you when they X-ray you, while they step behind a lead-lined wall. Over the years, and after numerous X-rays, the effect of the relatively low dosage can still damage your body.

If you receive a strong dose of radiation during a nuclear incident, you may find yourself losing your hair, vomiting blood, becoming extremely weak and disoriented, and perhaps dying within hours or days. If you receive a weak dosage, you may live for months or even many years, but you will find that your teeth and bones tend to decay, and you will be prone to cancer. This is the birthright of thousands of children born in Eastern Europe who lived beneath the path of the winds carrying the fallout from the Chernobyl nuclear power plant disaster.

Nuclear radiation is most dangerous immediately after a bomb is detonated. Much depends upon the nature of the radioactive material contained in the bomb. The fallout produced by the detonation of a typical bomb from the U.S. military arsenal will generate very powerful radiation for the first few hours. After a given period of time, a period known as the "half life" of the radioactive isotope, it will lose half its strength. After another equal period of time, it will lose half of its remaining strength, etc. So, during the Cuban Missile Crisis, we were told that we might be able to leave our fallout shelters and go outside in as little as two weeks from the time a bomb was detonated. Again, this depends upon how heavy the cloud of fallout is in your vicinity and how the "half lives" of the radioactive material are measured. Some are measured in hours or days, others are measured in thousands of years.

Dirty Bombs

One scenario anticipates the use of so-called dirty bombs. Dirty bombs are home made contraptions. The radioactive materials may be stolen from laboratories or hospital X-ray centers, and blown into tiny particles using readily available explosives such as dynamite. These weapons, though much smaller than conventional nuclear weapons, are very dangerous for two reasons. First, they can be set off in a highly congested part of a major city, spreading their radioactive materials over a few city blocks. Second, unlike a conventional nuclear weapon, the half-life of the radioactive material is measured in thousands of years. As a result, the contaminated area might be uninhabitable for many lifetimes. Terrorists might target a Federal Reserve facility in order to contaminate the money supply, or a major Internet or communications terminus in order to cripple traffic.

Under these circumstances, a fallout shelter would be useful only until the inhabitants could be evacuated, The occupants would want immediate access to potassium iodide tablets for themselves and, especially for any children. Children's thyroids more readily absorb certain deadly radioactive elements, posing the danger of cancer and other problems. Unfortunately, Potassium Iodide may not be effective against the radioactive isotopes released by a dirty bomb.

Power Plant Meltdowns

Having successfully targeted major structures with civilian airliners, it's reasonable to assume that terrorists would like to crash a plane into a nuclear power plant. They would hope for a reactor meltdown or the vaporization of the fuel rods stacked in the cooling tanks. This would result in tons of normally inert masonry and reinforcing rod being turned into deadly radioactive dust that would be drawn into the atmosphere. This airborne fallout would be swept from west to east, dropping out of the clouds and making areas of America uninhabitable while reducing the quality of life in the remainder. As these clouds moved eastward, they would pollute the soil and water, invade the food chain, and cause lasting harm to our population, just as the Chernobyl disaster affected the populations for thousands of miles from Belarus to Scandinavia. For that reason, Pripyat, in the Ukraine, once a thriving city of 45,000, now sits abandoned and crumbling.

Pripyat was the city nearest the Chernobyl reactor that began to melt down in April, 1986, burning dangerously for six months, as it spewed tons of cancer-causing isotopes into the atmosphere. These isotopes ultimately girded the globe, and although we did not receive large exposure in the United States, we did receive some. Downwind of Chernobyl, cow's milk is contaminated, the teeth of millions of children are rotting, and the population is far more prone to cancer. Everyone who inhaled the air, or ate any product of the soil, or drank the water, was in danger from the airborne contaminants that came to rest across Western Europe.

Conventional Nuclear Weapons

Worse, perhaps, is the news that Al Queda may have actually purchased a nuclear weapon on the black market. Considering the millions of tons of merchandise that move through our ports each day, it will not be difficult for them to secrete this weapon in a lead lined container to avoid detection, or to detonate it in a port city such as San Diego, New Orleans, Houston, or New York. If they successfully attack a west coast city, not only will they potentially kill millions of Americans, but a cloud of deadly radiation will sweep across our nation.

BIOLOGICAL WEAPONS

If there is a successful attack with a biological agent, it will expose every civilian's careless lack of preparation. Many Americans do not practice the simple habit of washing their hands after using the toilet. Many are casual in the way they handle food. Places that we go and people that we meet can easily become breeders and carriers of deadly disease.

If we all develop good habits of hygiene, we may limit the spread of the contagion and help stop a massive epidemic, thus saving many lives. When it comes to disease, the life you save may be your own!

If there is a bio-attack, and we panic and selfishly and ignorantly try to run away to escape it, we will spread the disease from city to city, taking it beyond the range and scope of emergency workers, and effectively killing ourselves and others. That's why current law permits authorities to shut down transportation corridors into and out of our cities. Emergency workers are prepared to close highways and shut down public transportation in order to keep contaminated individuals from spreading an infection to another community and creating an epidemic.

Under such circumstances, you will be well advised to isolate yourself and your loved ones in a safe room that is well stocked with food, water and medical supplies.

If millions followed these suggestions, it could result in a significant reduction in the number of lives lost.

There are numerous kinds of biological weapons, but most are not practical for terrorist use. For example, terrorists can attempt to infect or poison a municipal water supply, but since the amount of water processed is so enormous, they would need an enormous quantity of the toxin. What's more, most water in open canals and resevoirs is routinely tested and treated with chlorine before distribution.

Terrorists are most likely to use anthrax, botulism, or smallpox. As a child of the 40s, I was immunized against smallpox, but that immunization has probably long since lost its effectiveness. In 1977, the last case of smallpox was reported anywhere in the world. Even so, many of us have wondered why the government discontinued that immunization program. Both smallpox and polio are again on the rise in the world.

With the increase of experimentation in deadly biological agents, smallpox once again becomes a concern to the peoples of the world, particularly the Third World. Several countries have been reported to have large military stockpiles of smallpox agents. The United States government, however, claims to have millions of doses of smallpox vaccine, primarily for our military, so it is possible that we might be able to neutralize any serious threat—at least to our military.

You don't need to be wearied with descriptions of other potential biological hazards. It is sufficient to know that at the first indication that a biological agent has been released in your area, you must take measures to protect yourself and your loved ones, and to get under cover immediately. If you have sufficient warning, you might pull on clothes that cover your entire body, especially your eyes, nose and mouth, and put on a SARs resistant surgical mask or a gas mask. The most important thing is to flee, then flush yourself off, remove your clothing, and flush yourself off again. Then get yourselves into a room where you can prevent these toxins from entering by using filtered air. If you believe that you have been infected, you may wish to isolate yourself from loved ones in order to keep them from becoming infected.

Chemical Weapons

Chemical weapons have been used for many centuries, generally as a means of assassination. During World War I, Mustard Gas was widely used, blinding its victims, burning their skin and destroying their lungs.

Today, many more sophisticated chemicals have been developed. Among these is Sarin, the gas that was successfully used to kill commuters in a terrorist attack on a Tokyo subway station.

The best way to deal with a chemical attack is to flee the scene, moving into the wind and away from the area. If you have a gas mask available—especially a self-contained unit—you might be okay. But many chemicals are absorbed into the blood through the skin, so it's dangerous to risk going into harm's way.

3. Terror's Opponents

CAN GOVERNMENT PROTECT YOU?

Since 9/11, many of us have been breathing an occasional sigh of relief and whispering, "So far, so good." At the same time, polls indicate that 76% of all Americans expect another major terrorist attack. Although our government is taking herculean measures to protect us, our leaders have been consistently warning us that another attack appears inevitable.

Some in our society have blamed our government for 9/11. Others blamed the builders of the World Trade Center. It seems that a lot of people in politics and the press fail to remember that it was a terrorist organization, bent on taking over the world, that succeeded in their second attacked on the Twin Towers and upon our people. Our leaders didn't steal the jetliners. The builders of the World Trade Center didn't dive those jetliners into the Twin Towers. The enemies of civilization committed that heinous crime.

Many are now demanding that the government that was unable to protect them from 9/11 somehow protect them from future terrorist attacks. Others expect government to provide instant relief in the event of any such similar catastrophe. That is unrealistic.

Terrorists are opportunists continually looking for vulnerabilities which they can exploit. It is the anticipation of that random act of terror made on some unsuspecting citizen in some unlikely place that evokes terror in our hearts. Next time, we realize, it could be us.

Consider the two men who recently traveled about in a car, sniping at people in gas stations and parking lots in Virginia. People in a three state area were afraid to get out of their automobiles to pump gas because of the fear of being shot to death by those men.

While it's true that we seem to be getting better at holding off the terrorists, it's also true that the terrorists are getting better at what they do. We can only hope that our elected officials, our law enforcement agencies, and our military will do their best to protect us. But whatever their success, it remains our responsibility to look out for ourselves.

Most politicians continue to put politics first. The recent 9/11 Congressional hearings became more of a platform for political infighting and finger pointing than an aid to the prevention of terrorism. In a vast land like the United States, with its thousands of miles of coastline and long international borders, we are highly vulnerable to terrorist attacks. It seems certain that, sooner or later, a dedicated, hate-filled enemy will again strike us.

The Y2K bug nearly overtook us with disaster before it was finally addressed by industry and government. While some argue that it was never a danger, it's clear that the real danger was neutralized exactly because concerned and knowledgeable people focused the public eye upon industry and government and compelled them to correct the problems before the clock struck twelve.

The four major electrical blackouts that have occurred over the past forty years are evidence that no corporation, administration, congress, court or agency has been willing or able to come to grips with this nation's electrical transmission problems.

It's very clear that our infrastructure is too vast and complex to preclude a potentially devastating enemy attack. The media has repeatedly reported how the simple day-to-day operations of computer communications, financial markets and electrical transmission systems have been interrupted by computer hackers, human error, defective equipment, and sheer overloading of the systems.

We cannot fairly expect our government to consistently and continually carry out the threefold task of protecting us from terrorist attacks, of effectively responding to such attacks, and of providing adequate and comprehensive assistance immediately following such attacks. Preparation is up to all of us.

CAN YOU RELY ON GOVERNMENT?

Do you rely on government to protect you from terrorism? The best led, best equipped, best prepared government in the world cannot guarantee this. Why? Because terrorists will strike where they are not expected.

Their target does not have to be large, costly or impressive. Nor do their weapons need to be sophisticated. It is enough that they hurt, maim or kill someone. That's why the bombing of a couple of passenger trains bullied the Spanish people into electing a government that would appease terrorism and resulted in Spain's withdrawing their troops from the U.S. led coalition in Iraq.

If you cannot be certain that our government can guarantee freedom from attack, can you really trust that same government to provide you with medical care, food or water immediately following such an attack? Of course not. Our emergency management people were well-prepared, forewarned, and on top of the recent hurricane disasters in Florida, but it still took time to come to the assistance of everyone who needed their help.

Our leaders are, for the most part, capable and conscientious, but they cannot foresee all possible scenarios and consequences. We recently lost half of our flu vaccine because of a lack of organization and oversight. So, even if the government stockpiles Cipro, smallpox vaccine, and potassium iodine for nuclear attack, they may not be able to effectively distribute them in time. They know that they cannot assure you of that sort of assistance. Sadly, able leaders like John Ashcroft, who possess great integrity and commitment, will find themselves vilified when attempting to protect our country.

The majority of Americans who are responsible for providing emergency services are conscientious, concerned, competent and courageous.

We should realize, however, that when disasters occur—such as 9/11, the 2004 Florida hurricane season, the 3-Mile Island reactor leak, or the Asian Tsunami disaster—it takes time for emergency personnel to respond. They must get to the scene, appraise the damage, plan their responses, transport needed supplies and personnel, and provide needed relief.

That's why the Federal Emergency Management (FEMA) website encourages every American to stockpile food, water and emergency equipment in preparations for such an attack.

Even in the case of the Florida hurricane disasters of 2004, where personnel were tracking the storms long before landfall—and with FEMA assisting the state emergency workers—it sometimes took days to get emergency food and water to isolated areas, and even weeks to restore vital electrical power.

If we imagine a catastrophe of unprecedented proportions occurring on U.S. soil, we must realize that emergency services themselves will be disrupted and that vital assistance—such as search and rescue teams, medical personnel, and the supplying of food and safe drinking water—may not be available for several days or even weeks. And you can only live a short time without food and water.

After the tsunamis struck Indonesia, Sumatra, Thailand, and other southeast Asian countries, tens of thousands of people fled inland and many perished because, two weeks after the disaster, emergency workers had still not been able to locate and assist them. For thousands who were injured and were suffering from dehydration, exposure and hunger, it was already too late.

In emergencies, we civilians are our own first line of defense. If all of us make some preparations, we may be able to survive for that one extra day that might be required before assistance can reach us. What's more, we may be the means to save friends and neighbors.

Immediately after 9/11, most people in America experienced a burst of patriotism and an accompanying determination to make personal sacrifices to assure our nation's survival. The individuals that the president selected to head Homeland Security and the Justice Department put aside politics for the best interests of the country.

The situation has changed. The persons who will head the Department of Homeland Security or the new combined security agency know that they are probably in a lose/lose scenario. One of them has the seemingly impossible task of combining 22 huge bureaucracies into one super agency. They are expected to keep America free of another major attack. If they succeed in this awesome responsibility, they will get relatively little glory or reward. If they fail, their careers could well be over.

Time line covering the two week period following the Asian tsunami

Asian Tsunami Recovery

9.0 Quake 120,000+ Dead	Tsunamis Flood Coasts	Millions thirst, Disease threat	Nations begin pledging relief; USA sends two naval fleets	USA Reps Tour; Meet to Plan	U.N. to Lead Relief Efforts	After 2 Weeks, Millions in Need
Christmas, 2004	Dec 26, 2004	Dec 27, 2004	Dec 29, 2004 – Jan 8, 2005	Jan 5, 2005	Jan 8, 2005	Jan 9, 2005

In spite of mobilization taking place on an international level, two weeks after the tsunami struck on December 25th, millions were still in need.

Government Responsibility

One responsibility of government is to protect us from attack and to defeat our enemies. President Bush has vowed to carry the war to our enemies, and to defeat them wherever they are found. Our government cannot reserve its prime military resources for rebuilding our infrastructure or to provide emergency management personnel for our citizens.

The attempted sinking of the U.S.S. Cole, the bombing of our marine barracks in Lebanon, and the attacks on our troops in Iraq, are a constant reminder that terrorists are targeting our nation's defenders. And if the enemy should become especially successful, they will seriously damage our ability to wage war. One thing is clear. We should not expect our men and women in uniform to show up at our homes the week after a terrorist attack to bring us food, water and medical supplies.

Community Responsibility

In times of disaster, emergency managers and community-based and faith-based organizations have long held certain traditional roles. CBOs and FBOs are set up to deploy volunteers and services for disaster relief and recovery. They organize volunteer resources, distribute food, water and other supplies, and provide human warmth and comfort.

Federal emergency managers, on the other hand, are typically focused on emergency operations and technical solutions. They are burdened with too much to do with too few resources. In many cases, they have their hands full simply maintaining a decent state of preparedness and responding when disaster occurs. As a result, they must work with volunteers in well-defined circumstances during and after disasters.

According to FEMA, the Community-Based and Faith-Based organizations have enormous strengths, including:

- Access to governmental expertise, technical know-how and funding.
- Large numbers of volunteers
- Understanding of community needs and an awareness of vulnerable populations
- Credibility within the community
- Access to social, religious, and ethnic groups that otherwise avoid interaction with government officials
- Ability to persuade and influence the community
- Power to make decisions outside government processes

Emergency managers provide access to:

- Understanding of local risks and preventative needs
- Current knowledge of status of relief in the community
- Ability to access and coordinate government expertise and resources at the local, state, regional and federal level

Billions of dollars and millions of hours are being invested to help local emergency agencies prepare for terrorist attacks. If these people and their resources aren't themselves injured in a massive terrorist attack, it remains that they will have their hands full meeting the needs of all those who are injured and who are without food, clothing and shelter.

Your Responsibility

If a terrorist attack of some kind strikes your town, and authorities are unable to visit your house for at least a week, what will they discover? After the 2004 hurricanes, emergency workers found terrible damage and many dead.

You may live in a rural area, and be confident that you will not be hurt by a terrorist attack. What will happen to you if transportation, electrical power, and communications are disrupted? Suppose food cannot be delivered to your area grocery stores. Suppose you can't pump water from your well. Will you be able to survive?

When enough people are well prepared, the number of deaths is reduced. In fact, individuals who are well prepared are no longer waiting for help but are prepared to help others.

It is your responsibility, as much as it lies within you, to protect yourself and to assist others.

If you prepare yourself for an attack, you become part of the solution rather than part of the problem. You frustrate terrorism. You become a citizen soldier akin to the spirit of '76.

4. Triumphing over Terror

Most of us have smoke detectors and fire extinguishers in our homes. Our local fire departments advise us to conduct home fire drills. We buy fire insurance. We try to keep first aid kits and flashlights somewhere in the house.

We assume bad things can happen, but we do all that we reasonably can to prevent and mitigate damages.

We also buy auto, life and health insurance. We carry spare tires and jacks and signal flares in our cars.

We may even keep some extra groceries and bottled water around in case our community is crippled by a hurricane, tornado, ice storm, flood or earthquake.

In fact, we scarcely notice how many things we do to protect our homes and families. We simply do them, and they provide a certain peace of mind. We don't live in fear.

So what's the big deal about taking a little extra effort to limit terrorism's danger to us? It's simple enough. All we need to do is take a few steps in addition to the other preventative measures that we already take against fire, crime and natural disasters.

The purpose of terrorists is to terrorize you. If we don't face them down, they will keep coming back, and each time they return they will be armed with more power.

George W. Bush is the international equivalent of Gary Cooper in the movie, "High Noon." He is determined to face the evil whether anyone helps him or not, at whatever the cost. He is attempting to save modern civilization in spite of the greed, obstructionism and cowardice demonstrated by many.

As individuals and as a nation, we are all always at risk. A natural disaster may overtake us at any time, destroying our homes, businesses, and communities. Other nations and peoples are filled with envy and jealousy and look on us with rapacious eyes. Our very success makes us a target.

Throughout history, the race has been subject to wars, disease and famine. Any catastrophe has elements of terror, whether natural or man made. In our day, however, a new factor has been added to the equation—systematic terror to achieve political power.

Our government's greatest challenge is to keep our enemies from using WMDs on our soil. This is best achieved by carrying the war to the their doorstep. The best defense remains a good offense. If the terrorists are running for their lives, it is nearly impossible for them to be recruiting and training additional terrorists, let alone managing to finance, equip, and communicate with their existing agents. We must continue to be proactive in this matter.

Finally, we must be prepared for what may be the inevitability of another atrocity on American soil. Such an attack is not unthinkable. We've already experienced several. Criminals like Bin Laden continue to threaten even more heinous assaults.

YOUR GREAT CHALLENGE

Your part in planning and preparing for such an event is covered in the following chapters.

In preparation for many types of attacks, including WMDs, the best thing that you can do is to prepare a place—a safe room— in your home, or apartment complex, and encourage similar preparations in schools, office buildings, shopping malls, office buildings and factories.

You need to be able to filter or seal out contaminated air and to shield yourself at least from low level radiation. And you must stockpile reasonable amounts of water, food and medical supplies so that you can maximize the likelihood of your survival. Finally, you must do this without bankrupting yourself or causing unnecessary anxiety to those around you during the months or years of anticipation and waiting.

It is not enough to have emergency services such as fire and police departments equipped and trained for terrorist attacks. Those who are charged with emergency management may be met with catastrophes in which hundreds, thousands, perhaps even millions of Americans will be injured or killed. While most of us hope that we will not be among the victims, we dare not presume on such good fortune. You must prepare.

Those who refuse to prepare for their own survival can only hope that emergency management people will be able to visit their disaster sites, assess the damage, lay the dead to rest, treat the injured, and feed and shelter the hungry within a day or two of any attack. Such a response is unlikely.

It's up to each of us to try to make certain that we, and those around us, are not killed in the first place. And it's up to each of us to survive for whatever period of time is required for help to arrive.

If you doubt this observation, you should check out the results of the relatively small nuclear bombings of Hiroshima and Nagasaki that ended World War II. Highly trained and equipped Japanese civil defense personnel were all but helpless to respond to those attacks. Yes, the use of nuclear weapons was unprecedented. It's sobering to realize that those devestating bombs were tiny compared to what might be used against us today.

Keep in mind, as well, how long it took the well-prepared and conscientious emergency management personnel to get water and ice to the victims of Hurricane Charley. And Hurricane Charley didn't leave behind radioactive debris or biological contaminants.

YOU CAN LIMIT TERROR'S IMPACT

You can join the battle against terrorism by becoming one of millions of Americans who are prepared not simply to care for themselves but who are also prepared to help lift the burdens of our government by coming to the aid of their neighbors.

You should have a simple and inexpensive shelter that is stocked for your survival, as well as a warning system to alert you. In addition, you should have at least minimal training to protect yourself and to provide care for your loved ones, and you should always carry on or near you various items that will promote your survival.

When you prepare yourself to survive terrorism, you inherently combat terrorists. You accomplish four things:

- First, you limit the damage that terrorists can cause.
- Second, you become an unofficial volunteer committed to assisting your neighbors in time of trouble—a good Samaritan.
- Third, you become part of an unofficial and unorganized army that helps head off attacks by reporting unusual activities.
- Fourth, you inhibit attacks by making terrorists realize that their extensive efforts may account for relatively little.

The best emergency management is that which is pursued at the local level. Each community best understands it's own infrastructure, it's population, it's strength and weaknesses, it's needs and it's resources. And the strongest communities are populated by responsible individuals who are ready to bear as much responsibility for themselves as they can.

This how-to book shows you how you can make a difference for God, family and country. It encourages you to do four things:

- Remain alert for and report possible terrorist activities.
- Prepare yourself and your loved ones to survive an attack.
- Equip yourself and your loved ones for its aftermath.
- Reach out in love by planning to help the less prepared to survive.

1. Remain Alert for Terror

It is every American's privilege to try to help prevent a terrorist attack. And while it may seem unlikely that you will have the opportunity to actually prevent an attack, some of us may. The FBI and the Department of Homeland Security rely on intelligence from extraordinary citizens like you and me.

You say, "I'll never really catch a terrorist!" But if millions of us remain alert and attentive, one or two will occasionally stumble onto some evidence of terrorist activity and may be able to contact authorities in time to prevent an attack. Some editorialists scoff at this idea, but we Americans know that similar programs—such as the Amber Alerts—really work. We simply need to be determined to do our part.

The FBI and the Department of Homeland Security encourage us all to report information concerning suspicious or criminal activity to the local FBI Joint Terrorism Task Force (JTTF). The FBI regional phone numbers can be found online at http://www.fbi.gov/contact/fo/fo.htm. The HSOC can be reached via telephone at 202-282-8101 or by e-mail at HSCenter@dhs.gov.

If you and every other American remains alert, the terrorists will always be looking over their shoulders to see whether they've been discovered. And they are far more likely to be exposed.

2. Survive an Attack

Your first goal should be to help prevent an attack.

Your second goal should be to survive an attack.

This book shows you how to assemble survival packs for each member of your family at prices that will not break your pocket book. If you will invest about a half an hour at your local discount store, you can fit out each family member with a pocket-size survival kit for less than five dollars each. Take a little more time and you can equip each of them with a much more comprehensive kit for about twenty dollars. Or furnish them with a very elaborate pack that meets FEMA recommendations for under $40 each.

You may not prevent a terrorist attack. It is very clear, however, that you have complete control over how you respond to it. You can study to prepare yourself for all manner of emergencies. You can acquire emergency equipment and supplies, and learn to use it. You can seek wisdom, strength and grace from God. These things will equip you to respond well, and the doing of them will encourage you and those around you. Your family will be pleased to see that you have a plan and that you are working that plan. It is far better than sitting around, moaning that you are a victim.

Individual Americans are justifiably uneasy about the necessity of relying upon our government to protect us from the consequences of terrorist attacks. The president of the United States cannot be at your workplace or in your living room the next time a terrorist attack is executed. He cannot hold your hand and guide you through your preparations and responses. As a matter of fact, neither can your state's governor, or your city's mayor, or your local policeman or firefighter. If there is a major disaster, emergency workers will get to you as soon as they possibly can. But they too may be struggling to survive, and they may have thousands of others clamoring for their attention. Remember that on 9/11 we lost a lot of brave police officers and fire fighters.

Our ancestors did not rely upon their government to grow their food, fetch their water, load their muskets, bandage their wounded, or bury their dead. They realized that, in a democracy, the elected officials are the representatives of the people, not their keepers. They abhorred the idea of a welfare state. They were a nation of volunteers, of citizen soldiers, of independent, hard-working people who cooperated with one another to ward off the consequences of any disaster, natural or man-made.

Yes, our infrastructure is far more complex today than it was at our nation's founding, but the wellbeing of each individual still remains his own concern and responsibility. Some imply that we are not smart enough to make value judgments or to care for ourselves. One moment they are telling women that they have the right to dictate their own reproductive destiny. They next moment they are telling those same women that they don't have the intelligence to manage their own retirement accounts. Truth is, those folks just want to dictate how we run our lives.

Are we less capable than our ancestors? They had character. They had soul. I believe that most Americans today also possess character. But a lot of us have forgotten our sacred responsibilities.

Your objective must be to help preserve and protect the lives of all Americans. Although you may not agree with all of the arguments in this book, they should be sufficient to support one conclusion, that every responsible citizen needs to prepare for survival.

3. Endure the Aftermath

Your third goal should be to stay alive and healthy during that period following an attack when you may have to rely upon yourself to persevere. Let's say that you escape a major hurricane or a terrorist attack without personal injury, but that your community suffers devastation. How will you survive the aftermath if government relief is not immediately available?

If you are willing to invest 24 hours and $240 to $480, this book will show you how to accumulate the supplies and equipment that your family of four will need to survive for up to two weeks in the aftermath of a major disaster. If you are responsible for more or less than four people, simply adjust the quantity of items you purchase to meet the needs.

4. Assist Others Less Blessed

Helping one's neighbor is as American as apple pie. It's this attitude that sets us apart from many other people who sell off their neighbors and friends to gain personal advantage. If you are well prepared, you may have it in your power to save the lives of others. In essence, you become as important as your local emergency workers by sharing some of their burdens. What's more, you may be first on the scene with the best means of helping.

It is your privilege and responsibility to carry as much of the burden for our own salvation as you are able. But it is also your responsibility to assist your neighbors.

When Jesus was asked, "What is the first commandment?" he quoted a passage from the Old Testament. He said, "Love the Lord your God with all your heart and with all your soul and with all your mind. This is the first and greatest commandment." He continued, "And the second is like it: Love your neighbor as yourself" (Matthew 22:37-39). This is the pivotal passage of scripture. You are to love God. You are to love yourself. You are to love your neighbor as yourself. He stated emphatically that it is more blessed to give than to receive. God blesses you in sometimes indiscernible ways because you have represented him well.

Ben Franklin, when signing the Declaration of Independence, put it in a less elegant way. "We must all hang together," he warned, "or, most assuredly, we shall all hang separately."

YOUR WINDOW OF OPPORTUNITY

The second major attack on U.S. soil has not yet occurred. God willing, it never shall. But there has been much horror in the history of the world. And it is clear that thousands of terrorists are dedicated to bring horror to our shores. In fact, it's estimated that there may be 5,000 terrorists on U.S. soil. Terrorism is a new and evil culture. It is effective in achieving its ends. It may be a popular means of political expression for a very long time.

You still have time to prepare.

This upbeat book provides specific, practical instructions for preparing yourself and your family against a terrorist attack, whether at home, work, school, shopping or on the road. It recommends inexpensive items that will promote survival, items that each family member should carry everywhere they go. These items may make the difference between life and death, between lifelong infirmity and good health.

Most of these preparations may be useful in surviving nearly every manner of disaster. They are equally helpful in surviving natural disasters, such as hurricanes and tornadoes, as well as terrorist attacks.

An obvious example is the possession of a generic pain reliever, such as aspirin. Whether one is dealing with the trauma of nuclear attack or the stress of fleeing a tornado, aspirin will be equally useful in limiting heart attack and stroke. Another example is a simple surgical mask that may protect one from inhaling dangerous agents as diverse as the anthrax bacillus, airborne particles from a burned or collapsed structure or radiological materials. A third example of a multi-purpose item is the sub-surface shelter used throughout the midwest to escape the wrath of tornadoes. Such a shelter may be adapted to protect from other threats, such as nuclear radiation. A knowledge of first aid will pay dividends whether you are treating a wound inflicted by a terrorist or treating a drowning victim using CPR.

This universality simplifies your preparations, reduces your investment in time and money, limits confusion, and increases your confidence.

Your Peace of Mind is your Responsibility

As you read this book, you are achieving three things. First, you are identifying potential dangers and how you might respond to them. Second, you are learning how to survive, and, hopefully, preparing emergency kits to weather the storms of adversity. Finally, you are gaining confidence that you are as prepared as possible—and more prepared than most—to survive. Foreknowledge of what you need to do in an emergency, and the confidence born of your preparation, will help you to remain calm and to communicate that spirit to those around you. You must stay as calm as possible so that you can help others and also keep your mind uncluttered as you strive to recognize and put to use things around you that might be useful in promoting survival.

If this advice is followed by a sufficient number of Americans, the outcome will be a stronger, more resilient nation, ready to quickly rebound from natural or man-made disasters of any kind.

As you prepare yourself to survive the difficult early days of an emergency, you will lift many of the burdens of our government, enabling it to redirect additional resources to the prevention of attacks, the apprehension of perpetrators, the provision of emergency services, the successful treatment of injured people, and the rapid reconstruction of damaged areas. As a result, we will become a more confident, better prepared, and more resilient nation.

BE PREPARED

We should all embrace the motto of the Boy Scouts of America, "Be prepared." It is a certain that more people would have escaped from the collapse of the World Trade Center if they had previously undergone emergency training, had possessed simple survival kits, and had been able to receive better information about what was occurring above or below the floors on which they worked.

One of the most horrible memories we have of the terrorist attack is that of people throwing themselves from the building in preference to being burned alive. If they'd had some rope in their desks, they might have been able to work their way down a floor at a time. Admittedly, it sounds like an unrealistic and a terrifying suggestion. On the other hand, it was a far more terrifying decision to leap nearly a thousand feet to their deaths. If the victims had portable radios at their desks, they might have learned in time that their buildings had been struck by airliners flown by terrorists, and they might have begun their escape down the stairs. Many did start to evacuate, but were misled, and thought it was okay to return to their desks. They did not again attempt to escape until it was too late.

Some clearly were overcome by fire, smoke and fumes. If they had carried gas masks, or even nuisance dust masks and goggles, to keep the acrid smoke from their lungs and eyes, they might have been able to fight their way through some of the smoky stairways to safety. But they didn't have these things. They lacked information. They lacked preparation. They lacked survival tools.

Of course, everyone couldn't escape. But a few inexpensive preparations might have increased the number of survivors. Isn't your life worth five bucks worth of preparation?

Throughout history people have lived in fear. There are a number of things that you can do to head off and overcome the effects of fear. Preparing for the unexpected is one of them. Your preparation is a service to society. It is nothing more than society has found necessary throughout history. It's not unlike hanging a fire extinguisher on your kitchen wall. Hopefully you will never experience a fire, but, if you do, you have taken some inexpensive precautions.

Preparation for Terror Starts with Simple Things

Some may rely on others to make their preparations for them. Others will prepare for themselves without caring what happens to their neighbors. One or two of your neighbors may prove to be opportunists, looters who attempt to take advantage of the misfortunes of others. Many will prepare so that they can help themselves, and not be dependent on others. And a few very special people—perhaps you—will prepare so that they can help both themselves and their neighbors.

Keep Terror in Perspective

Throughout history, people have had to take refuge from terror.

Nearly 2,000 years ago, the Christians of Rome lived deep among the many miles of tunnels that comprised the catacombs. The bones of many thousands are heaped there. Similarly, many troglodytes in France lived in caves below the earth's surface in order to escape religious persecution.

Our early-American forefathers hung their rifles over the doors of their cabins, ever ready to protect themselves from savagery. And they were forced to work their fields with weapons by their sides. During the Civil War, people on both sides buried food and precious possessions about their land so that marauding raiders might not find it.

During World War II, we planted Victory Gardens in our back yards. As a four-year old, I was disciplined by my mother for opening the black out curtain that covered our kitchen window. The English built backyard bomb shelters.

During the 1950s, during the Cold War, American school kids learned to duck and cover when the air raid whistle blew.

In the American mid-west and south, people still wisely build tornado cellars in their basements and back yards. In the southeast United States, new homes are often constructed with concrete "Safe Rooms" at their hearts to protect from hurricanes and other dangers.

The current administration has done a remarkable job of holding back the "inevitable" terrorist attack that most experts anticipate will dwarf earlier attacks in terms of scope of damage, number of casualties and recovery costs. Now it's time for each of us to carry our own small loads!

Step 2,
Plan for the Unexpected

5. The Planning Pack

PLAN YOUR ESCAPE

Prior to any emergency, you must make your family as aware as possible of the challenges they may face and the decisions that each member may have to make independently. You should familiarize them with the equipment you are providing them, and how they should use it to respond to various threats.

Hunker Down or Run for It?

In the event of an emergency, you and every family member must understand when they should remain where they are (shelter in place) and when they should attempt to return home or to some other prearranged location or rendezvous.

CONSIDERATIONS IN DECISION MAKING

Maturity Levels

Take the time to speak at length with your children about such matters. They are aware of many dangers. There "little minds" pick up far more than you are aware of. Indeed, the books they read and the TV shows they watch lead them to believe that it is a very dangerous world. Assess their temperament and maturity. Ask them their opinions on how they might react in different situations. Then offer your own suggestions. It is no secret that most children and teenagers love action adventures. Encourage your children to become independent thinkers. Sure, when you are with them, you can dictate. But you need to make them independent thinkers so that they can make vital decisions when you are not able to be with them.

Restricted Movement

In the case of adults, only police, the National Guard, and emergency workers have any right to restrict your movement. Keep in mind, however, that school authorities have legal obligations and rights to protect your children. They are acting *in loco parentis* (in the place of the parent), and may therefore be reluctant to let your children leave the facility. If you are relying upon an older, more mature student to help the younger reach a rendezvous, they may have to defy authority in order to carry out your instructions. Your child may or may not have up-to-date and accurate information about the situation.

If your children have a radio, they may actually be able to help the school authorities better understand what is happening. Having shared that information, however, you should be reluctant to encourage your teenager to defy the authority of school officials who, it is hoped, should have far more mature judgment. Obviously, if your children are safer at school than en route home, they should remain there. If the character of the emergency is such that school authorities are incapacitated or no longer able or willing to provide leadership, your children must decide whether it's safer to remain under their own supervision at the school or to head home. It's clear from the debacle at the 2004 Chechnyan school massacre that the adults and teachers were of little help in preserving life.

Communications Failures

It is in the midst of an actual attack that the cellular phone becomes important in making such decisions. You will need and want to speak with family members. But, if cellular systems are down or are swamped with calls, you won't get through. Walkie-talkies, with a range of several miles, are one alternative. A rigid set of written guidelines describing where your children are to attempt to go under various circumstances is an excellent fallback if communications fail.

Worst Case Scenario

These are frightening deliberations. Do not allow yourself to be paralyzed by doubt or fear. You may find yourself in a situation where you cannot get to your children to assist them. You may feel that they cannot make decisions or that they lack the capacity to succeed. This notwithstanding, you must have a rendezvous to which they can make their way, or you must find a way to get to them. Perhaps your child's pre- school building is where you should have your family meet if they cannot get home. But, if the unspeakable occurs, and the attack centers near their pre-school, you may not be able to reach them.

This may sound cold blooded, but, in the event of a general attack, you must make up your mind to attend to the needs of the majority of your family. Then, and only then, dare you risk taking steps to locate the missing. For as long as you are able, try to treat it as though it is all "make believe," a sort of game. Your kids probably play some pretty violent video computer games, yet they seem able to separate the fantasy from the real world. You must treat terrorism in a similar manner. Finally, demonstrate your leadership and confidence by always remaining calm and by teaching your children to pray to and rely upon God.

ESTABLISHING PLACES OF RENDEZVOUS

Establish meeting places at which you may rendezvous. Home is, of course, the most desirable place because it contains many of the things you might require in an emergency, including shelter, food, water, blankets, clothing, and much more.

If your children learn that they cannot or should not return home because it is severely damaged or because the area is contaminated, they should know how to make their way to an alternate prearranged rendezvous. If you select two or three places of rendezvous, the family can pick one that is furthest from the terror incident and therefore safer.

You must consider the character of the threat. Do you live near a nuclear power plant or an oil refinery, or does your home lie below a major dam or in a low-lying area beneath a levy? You'll want to get away from such areas of danger.

Prepare a list of names, addresses and phone numbers of trusted friends and relatives with whom your family might stay. List these on the smallest piece of paper on which you can fit them, then draw a map on the reverse side. Make a copy for each family member to carry in their survival packs, print an extra copy for each automobile, and print one copy for each friend and relative listed so that they will know where you might try to go if you are unable to reach them.

PREPARING MAP PACKS

Map One

Acquire a detailed map of the area covering your home, places of work, schools, etc. This map might show your city, your entire county, or just your neighborhood. With your home as the center of interest, use a compass to draw a circle that includes, if possible, your children's schools, their friend's homes, shopping malls, and any nearby work places. Cut away the part of the map that displays these places and discard the remainder. Take it to a copy center and reduce or enlarge it to the size of a sheet of paper, 8 1/2" X 11". Make a copy for each member of your family.

Now, using colored high liters to designate roads and pathways, mark each map so that it is custom-designed for a particular member of your family. For example, if it's for your 16-year old, and she ordinarily walks to school, trace the route from home to school with a yellow high liter. Now, if there is an alternative route, mark it in another color. You might use yellow for the preferred route, red for an alternate route, etc. Do the same to show how she can get home from a friend's, from the store, or from a part-time job. Do not assume that, because a person is an adult, they do not need the map. If they should be injured or suffer shock, someone else may refer to the map to help them find their way.

Create a custom map for each member of your family. Print their name at the top in bold letters, along with your home address and home and cell phone numbers.

Realize, however, that family members may not be able to get home because their movements are restricted. Establish alternative points of rendezvous and prioritize them by putting letters or numbers on the map, so that each one knows that, if they can't get home, they are to go to point A, and if they can't go to point A, they are to go to point B.

Point A and point B may represent the home of a friend or relative, or even the parking lot of a shopping mall. Whenever you establish these points, try to avoid places where crowds may gather. And keep in mind that you may not be able to remain uncovered or out of doors because of dangers from WMDs.

Sound scary? It should. During time of war, families are often divided. Lives are changed. We cannot sugar coat the possibilities. The better prepared you are, the more likely you are to be quickly reunited with your loved ones. There is one other thing that you can and should do. You should pray that the Lord keeps you and your loved ones safe, that he gives you wisdom and strength and brings you together again.

Map Two

Map two is a larger scale map, covering a radius of fifty or one hundred miles, and perhaps even more.

Again, with your home at the center, use a compass to draw a circle whose radius takes in the homes of trusted friends and relatives, even if they live in neighboring states.

Again, using a color marker, highlight the high-speed routes to each home. You should also mark an alternative route because the main highways will very likely become congested or blocked. Incidentally, your teen children may actually reach their destination faster riding a bicycle than you can in a car because of highway congestion.

Where possible, everyone should plan to travel as part of the group to avoid predators. Along each route, mark several landmarks that are familiar to all but the youngest family members, including restaurants, service stations, shopping malls, campgrounds, and other potential shelters and sources of food.

On the periphery of the map, print the names, addresses and phone numbers of the places marked as destinations. Draw a straight line from each destination to that block of information.

Now, square off the corners of the portion of the map that you've market up, take it to a local copy center, and reduce it to 8 1/2" x 11". Again, make a copy for each member of your family, a copy for each vehicle, and copies for each trusted friend and family member to whose house you might travel in the event of an emergency.

Combined and Laminated Maps

Take one copy of the customized LOCAL map that indicates routes from work or school to your home, and paste it back-to-back with one of the large-scale evacuation maps from the second set. Make a set of maps for each family member, one for each vehicle, and one for each of the trusted friends and family whom you might visit. This way, you have a record of what route each person is to attempt under varying conditions. To protect these maps, have a local copy center laminate them.

Put a copy of each map in the emergency pack of the family member for whom you designed it, put copies in each auto glove compartment, and send the rest on to the trusted friends at potential destinations.

You may in turn receive copies of similar maps made by friends and loved ones who might come your way if the emergency is in their location rather than yours. Put these maps in a safe place in car or home.

IDENTIFICATION

It's also a good idea to have a number of snapshots of each family member. Put each one's name, address, and phone number on the back of their respective photo. Use a rubber stamp ink pad to put their thumb and index finger prints on the back, then add their blood type, any medical problems or medications required, their date of birth, height, weight, hair color, and any distinguishing marks, so that you can provide this record to emergency workers in the even that you are separated.

DRY RUNS

The next time you decide to visit one of the friends or relatives who has agreed to host you in time of emergency, make it a point to leave home early to permit more time for the journey. Along the way, point out places, such as service stations and restaurants, where family members might improvise a shelter. Stop every few miles at some easily recognizable place so that you can drill your family on its location, appearance, relative distance from the previous point, and decide upon the safest place to stay if they are allowed within the building.

6. The Communications Pack

THE CELLULAR PHONE

Don't Leave Home Without It!

We're not referring to a credit card here. We're talking about your ability to talk to emergency personnel, family members and friends. We're talking about a cellular telephone. Cell phones saved lives on 9/11. Don't leave home without it!

The Body Needs Cells

Get one for every member of your family who is mature enough to use it. The cellular phone is vital for a number of reasons.

The phone may be used to alert authorities to real or possible threats. Additionally, any family member or friend may call others to warn them of a real or potential attack of which they have been warned or in which they find themselves involved. The phone may also be used to call authorities or family members for assistance.

And, in the event of an attack, your family may use the phone to alter rendezvous plans.

Finally, the phone can be used to instruct family or friends to bring additional or alternative items to the rendezvous or evacuation point.

You can buy a cellular phone and operate it for as little as $20 per month, and you can set up family calling plans, with a walkie-talkie feature, for less than $20 per person per month.

The Cellular Survival Pack

The cellular telephone might be classified as a survival pack in and of itself. With it, you can call for help, communicate and rendezvous with others, and keep in contact with the world.

Effective communications are vital to your safety and happiness. On 9/11 people were saved from the incredible wreckage of the Twin Towers because they were able to communicate by cellular phone. In addition, we've learned that heroic airline passengers were able to surreptitiously use their cellular phones to reach family members and governmental authorities.

This incredible marvel of modern technology is the single most important piece of communications equipment you can possess. It should maintain its usefulness in all but a general nuclear attack. In that case, electronic waves created by the bomb's detonation could interfere with singals and destroy delicate digital signaling and storage devices. Its effect upon you will also depend upon how close you are to the raditaion that it produces.

FAMILY PHONE POLICY

Program each cell phone with the numbers of:

- Immediate family members
- Friends and relatives who have committed themselves to host or assist you
- Emergency organizations

Remember that the "911" emergency service may be overwhelmed with calls during a crisis. It may be meaningful to have the direct number of your local ambulance service, and fire and police departments programmed as well.

Teach everyone in your family how to use these phones. Impress on them the importance of not using the phones frivolously and of keeping the batteries charged. Make certain they carry their phones wherever the go. Teach them cell phone courtesy, to shut them off or mute them during classes, meetings, and while at church or in an audience. Cell phones are not always welcome in schools because they are considered a distraction and, worse, even a means of negotiating drug sales. Many employers like to bar them because they are perceived not only as a distraction but as a device for industrial espionage. Be prepared to contend with those in authority because cellular phones can also save lives and property, perhaps theirs.

WALKIE TALKIES

These devices, effective up to several miles, have become very inexpensive. You might consider putting a walkie talkie in the survival pack of each family member, instructing them as to the preferred and alternative channel settings that should be used to communicate with family members. At least one cellular service provider offers a walkie talkie feature on its cell phones.

LOW-TECH COMMUNICATIONS

Other means of communication that should not be ignored are low-tech, and for that reason are in many ways more reliable. Anyone who watched the movie, "Titanic," recognizes that a whistle can be of great value to someone who needs to be rescued. Add to that a small hand- held cosmetic mirror for reflecting sunlight in order to get attention. And don't denigrate the lowly match or cigarette lighter. Sophisticated search gear carried on an airplane detected the striking of a match by a man who had been lost in a blizzard. He was several miles away from the searching aircraft, in a mountainous area, it was nighttime, and snow was falling. Finally, a pen and paper provide a great means for leaving notes that can be stuck up in obvious places at home, on the back of a sign or on bulletin board or an agreed on place at a designated rendezvous.

DEMAND GOVERNMENT WARNING SYSTEMS

Our government has failed to institute two very simple, inexpensive and effective programs for warning Americans of immediate threats to their safety. The first program is a system that uses existing electrical transmission lines to send warning signals to our homes, schools and workplaces that activates an inexpensive device plugged into an electrical outlet. The second program is a system whereby thousands and even millions of phones can be rung simultaneously so that a terrorist alert can be delivered in a matter of seconds. Such a system could save your life.

Consider calling or writing your Congressman or Senator to get action on these matters.

7. The Assets Pack

CACHE CASH

None of us, of course, wants to hide cash in the mattress or sugar bowl if it might be earning interest. On the other hand, we know that major electronic banking systems have been shut down, and millions of people have been inconvenienced for extended periods, because skillful criminals successfully hacked their electronic systems. We also know that certain kinds of attacks, such as that on the World Trade Center, can destroy banking and communications networks. And we know that power failures and interruptions to the Internet may result in the inability of banks to transact business. In such a situation, you will be unable to use your credit cards or to access money through an ATM during and following a major terrorist attack. It's therefore vital that you set aside cash for a "rainy day."

Keep Cash On Hand

If you can afford it, and can securely do so, hide away some cash along with the family records you will take with you during an emergency. Better yet, carry some extra cash with you at all times, because you never know when you may need it.

Look at it this way. If you lose your job, or have a financial emergency, then you've set this money aside for just such a rainy day. But don't use it frivolously because you may find yourself smack dab in the middle of a real terrorist emergency (or in bankrupcy court).

How much is enough?

How much emergency cash should you have on hand? The answer depends upon how well off you are and how able you are to do so.

Your goal should be to set aside enough cash to pay for a one week road trip for your family. You should be prepared to pay cash for gasoline, food and housing for at least a week. A few years ago, a couple was left without heat or lights in their Charlotte home when an ice storm took down power lines and left a million customers without power. They picked up and drove south 100 miles where they took a motel room for a day to get warm. It costs money to travel.

Keep in mind that some businesses will engage in illegal predatory pricing. If you are already living hand-to-mouth, set aside the bare minimum that, in your situation, you are able to spare. Make certain that your children have at least enough money to make one phone call, or to catch the subway out of the city limits, or to buy a burger and a milk. Even a couple of bucks each could proved vital. But of course you must make your children understand that this money is sacred and is only to be used for a true emergency.

Avoid the refrigerator

You need to be clever in how you hide that cash away, and you need to impress upon your family the importance of "forgetting" that they have it available until such time as they may need it.

Most thieves know that people hide cash in the refrigerator because it is more or less fireproof. Some people, however, still put it in a plastic bag and hide it in a coffee can in the back of the refrigerator. A dedicated thief, with sufficient time, will simply pour things out on the floor until he finds your money.

Others hide money in fire resistant storage boxes, but these are easily identified and broken into. If you are handy, you might build a hidey hole beneath or behind a book case or in a closet where you can place one of these boxes. Or, you might get a wall safe. It's not a good idea to hide money behind a brick in a chimney because someone may start a fire in the fireplace. If you have an old cellar, you can probably find a dozen places that a thief would have difficulty locating. But you might also have difficulty locating the money if the lights are out and you're in a hurry. Keep it in as convenient a place as possible. Some have take a section of waterproof PVC pipe, capped one end, put a screw cap on the other end, inserted valuables, and buried it in the back yard. But you'd better make certain that your neighbors don't see you doing it.

Your biggest problem with hiding money isn't the fear of fire. If the house burns, and you haven't gotten home first to get the money, you have bigger problems than simply losing the emergency cash. A warning: If you must share with your children where you have hidden the cash, you are at high risk that an immature child will in turn share that delicious secret with a special friend. As soon as a second person knows a "secret," it is no longer a secret.

And you won't want your daughter picking up a cool new CD, or your husband buying you last minute flowers with the money that's been allocated for an emergency. Or you, yourself, being tempted to buy something that catches your eye. These cash reserves must be considered sacred to your survival.

Okay, you should try to have enough cash on hand to buy meals for at least a week, to pay the cost of a motel for six or seven nights, and to purchase gas for your car. Of course, there may be no motel rooms available at any price, the restaurants may be closed, and the pumps shut down. So, you should have enough cash to buy whatever you can get that will help. More importantly, you should have most of the things that you might need stored away in anticipation of an emergency. This includes food, clothing, perhaps camping gear, and even a can or two of gasoline.

> **Warning**. A gallon of gas can generate an explosion equivalent to a several sticks of dynamite. Be careful where you store and how you carry gasoline.

Fake Them Out

A man I knew carried two wallets. One contained a small amount of spending money along with an outdated driver's license and other valid looking cards. That wallet was carried in his rear pocket and was used for regular purchases, such as meals and gasoline. A second wallet was kept in a front pocket and contained valid documents and a substantial sum of money. A pickpocket would, of course, go for the obvious wallet in the back pocket. If approached by a mugger, he would have offered him the "dummy" wallet from his back pocket. He also wore a reliable but inexpensive wrist watch, and dressed in flannel shirts (with ties) and nice slacks. That was an advantage that he enjoyed as an eccentric and wealthy entrepreneur. He did not appear to be worth robbing. And he generally drove a pickup truck unless he was taking his family out.

Cash Only Policies

In the event of an attack, cash may be your only means of exchange. But if America's muggers learn that millions of people are carrying around extra cash, there may be a rash of attacks. If your money is hidden away in a wall safe at home, but you are at the mall when an attack occurs, the money won't do you much good. When an emergency occurs, every family member should have a portion of that cash with them in case they become separated from one another. In the case of little children, it can be sewn into their coat, or under the padding in their sneakers, while adults might carry it in a money belt

You can carry a money belt everyday. There are two kinds.

One is made of nylon, and has sufficient space to store a passport, credit cards and cash. It may be hung about your neck beneath your shirt or blouse, or about your waist beneath your clothes. Carry extra cash, ID, and other vital items in the money belt.

The other is a real leather belt. The back of the belt has a zipper which provides access to a long narrow pouch adequate to carry a couple of hundred dollars. This belt looks like any other belt a man might wear.

For a few dollars, you might install a neat nook in your family car where you can salt away a few dollars more.

No matter how well hidden your money may be, a robber may challenge you for it. Don't lose your life trying to fight off a thief.

How About ATM and Credit Cards?

By all means, keep these important items with you. If cash should prove accessible through your bank or an ATM machine, you will have the cards at hand. If not, you will have protected the cards by carrying them with you.

OTHER VALUABLES

Examine Your Values

Do not lose your life because you take undue time trying to gather worldly possessions to take with you. You may one day accumulate more wealth. What possible good can you be to your loved ones if you lose your life? One cannot forget the lesson in "Indiana Jones and the Last Crusade," where the demi-heroine let herself fall into the abyss because she cared more about possessing the so-called holy grail than she cared for life itself. Keep your perspective.

Vital Documents

When you must leave home, whether because of a hurricane evacuation order or a terrorist attack, take copies of all of your vital documents with you. After each of the 2004 hurricanes, people returned to their neighborhoods wondering whether their homes would still be standing. Many lost everything, and most came to realize that a family photograph or a copy of an insurance policy often meant more than the family jewels. Make copies of precious documents while you have the leisure to look at the subject objectively. Pack them carefully in a stiff, waterproof envelope, or a couple of freezer bags, and have them ready to take with you.

- Passports
- Social Security Cards
- Birth Certificates
- Marriage Certificate
- Medical and inoculation records
- Most recent bank statement, showing balances
- Investment information
- Family photos
- Art work
- Keepsakes
- Official identification cards

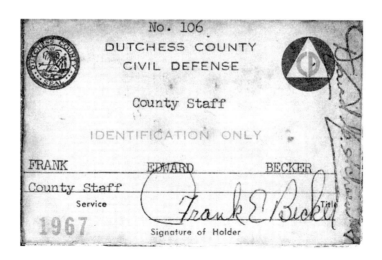

Real Estate Records

Financial counselors will generally assure you that your single most valuable asset is your house. That had better not be so. Your most precious "assets" are the people that you love and who love you in return. If you have no family, then you need to make some worthy friends.

This notwithstanding, your house should be pretty high on your list of material possessions. And, if it is, then you need to be able to prove that it is yours, as well as how much money you still owe the bankers for it, and how much you have it insured for. You need to safeguard a copy of your deed, your mortgage agreement, and your insurance policy because, when you return home, it may not be there.

Safe Deposit Box Keys

If you leave this at home, you may return to find it melted beneath a pile of ashes. Take it with you, in the safest place you can find.

Jewelry

Jewelry has both sentimental and cash value. It should not be left at home unless you have a secure and fireproof vault. If you do take it when you evacuate, do not carry it in your pocketbook or backpack. These are items that you might be separated from, or that might be separated from you. If you must take jewelry, do not wear it. The exception is a simple wedding band.

Do not attract unnecessary attention. If you feel that you must take jewelry, put it in the inside zippered pocket of a jacket, or some similar place. If necessary, divide it between your companions so that you "Don't keep all your eggs in one basket."

One man had a tailor sow zippered pockets into the inside of his pant legs, below the calves, and he carried important items there.

Remember, none of these things is as important as your life and the lives of your loved ones. You are escaping to preserve lives. Don't wind up sacrificing those lives for something of far less value.

STEP 3,
Procure Survival Supplies

8. The Pocket Pack

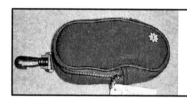

	Pocket Pack
	Weight, 5 1/2 ounces
	Investment, $5 to $10

BASIC SURVIVAL KIT

The following chapters describe three first response survival packs that are both personal and portable. These very small kits are designed to increase the likelihood of your survival in the midst of, or immediately following, a terrorist attack. They may also provide minimal food and water to keep you going for a day or two.

The Pocket Pack may be hung from your belt or carried in a purse, backpack, or even a pocket. It is the most elementary and vital item in your survival kit. It is proof once again that "Good things come in small packages." It contains four basic survival tools that should provide great peace of mind.

You should have the Pocket Pack nearby at all times, whether sleeping or awake. This cannot be overemphasized. It will do you little good if you are find yourself in the middle of an emergency and realize that you left it at home on your dressing table or in your car's glove compartment. This could be a matter of life and death.

The Pocket Pack is designed to be carried by all individuals above the age of three or four. It consists of minimal but vital survival equipment. As opportunity permits, you may set up larger and more comprehensive survival packs.

Every parent that has the means should make certain that each family member carries one. You should be able to assemble one of these kits for between four and eight dollars.

POCKET PACK CONTAINERS

The container that you use to hold these four items may consist of something as simple as a zip lock sandwich bag or an oversize traveler's plastic soap container. The over-size traveler's soap dish has a number of advantages. It has a hard shell, is uniform in shape, and is inexpensive. On the downside, it should be wrapped with a rubber band to keep it from slipping open, and it has to be carried in a pocket to purse.

Pocket Packs® containing surgical mask, gloves, space blanket, & goggles

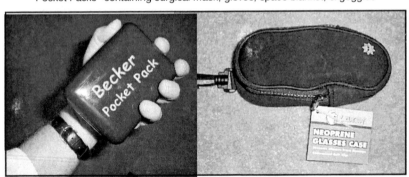

As an alternative, you might consider using an oversize Neoprene Glasses Case, sold at large discount stores. It has a convenient zipper, and can be worn at the waist by hooking it to your belt or a belt loop.

You might also consider a canvas shotgun Choke Tube Case, purchased in the sporting goods department, that can also be worn on your belt.

You can position either of these toward the small of your back where a sweater, suit coat, or wind breaker will cover them nicely.

While you may think of a half dozen other containers that will serve as well, keep in mind that they must be approximately 1 1/4" deep by 3" x 4" in order to carry the required items.

The advantage of the belt mounted case is that is stays with you throughout the day and you are unlikely to set it down and find yourself without it in the midst of an emergency.

Eye glass case makes excellent Pocket Pack

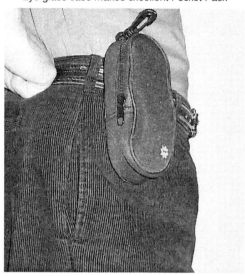

We civilians do not have access to the protective over garments used by the military to protect against biological and chemical attack. The military has special boots, plus M40 Protective Masks and chemical and biological resistant gloves.

You can, however, purchase several inexpensive items that will improve your chances of survival against the three age-old enemies that accompany many terrorist attacks—fire, smoke and dust. What's more, some of these available off-the-shelf items may provide significant protection against biological toxins, such as anthrax.

Although the Pocket Pack contains only four items, these items are considered most promising in dealing with a variety of terror attacks. The Pocket Pack contains one or two surgical masks, one pair swimming goggles, two surgical gloves, and one emergency foil "space" blanket.

Important note: Your particular physical condition, age, and location may cause you to alter the contents of the Pocket-Pack. For example, someone with a heart problem might substitute a prescription drug or a couple of aspirin tablets for one of these items.

THE POCKET PACK'S CONTENTS

A plastic sandwich bag may also serve as a Pocket Pack container

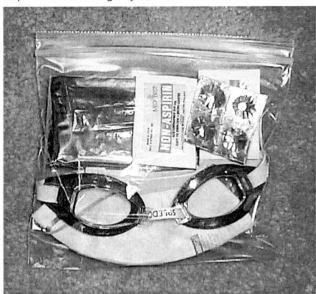

The items in the Pocket Pack are so compact that they fit in a soap dish or a sandwich baggy. In fact, each of the items shown above are all still in their original display packages. Once they are removed from their blister packs, they require even less space. The swimming goggles, however, should be kept in a separate plastic sandwich baggy to protect the lenses from scratches.

The four primary items include:

- Surgical or nuisance dust mask
- Surgical gloves
- Swimming goggles
- Emergency foil-coated "space" blanket.

Surgical and Nuisance Dust Masks

Nuisance Dust Masks

In the event of a terrorist attack, even a simple nuisance dust mask may prove a lifesaver. This is especially true for those prone to heart or lung disease, as well as for asthmatics and allergy sufferers.

The idea is to keep those tiny particles of dirt and debris floating around in the air from getting inside your lungs.

Nuisance Dust Mask

A nuisance dust mask appears to have very limited usefulness. In fact, if you are not familiar with the potential dangers, your reliance upon a nuisance dust mask may prove catastrophic. A well-constructed nuisance dust mask, however, will reduce the amount of dust and other airborne particulates inhaled into your sinus tract and lungs. And, if you tape the edges of the mask so that all air entering your lungs must pass through the mask, you are obviously reducing dangerous material from entering your lungs and bloodstream.

If you recall the photographs of escaping victims and rescue workers from the falling Twin Towers on 9/11, you will envision people whose hair was thick with dirt and whose faces were unrecognizable because their eyes, ears and mouths were caked with dirt. Now, three years later, many of those people have been diagnosed with lung problems that may have resulted from breathing those largely undetermined particulates.

Civilians escaping from the twin towers, as well as those on the streets below, covered their noses and mouths with whatever they could find to keep smoke and dust out of their respiratory tracts. They used shirtsleeves, handkerchiefs, facial tissues, and, if they were better prepared, nuisance dust masks.

Obviously, even a simple and well-constructed dust mask would have helped reduce the inhalation of these dangerous materials that included toxins, asbestos and other cancer-causing carcinogens, as well as powdered glass and masonry.

The clouds of dirt that fouled the air, choked the lungs, and blinded the eyes was an aggregate that contained many dangerous components, including hydrocarbons, soot, metals and metallic salts—even perhaps some radioactive residue, common in our atmosphere—plus asbestos particles and other dangerous elements. Those few who had dust masks did not entirely escape the pollution, but they definitely reduced the amount of dust inhaled. As a result, those who had face masks experienced a reduction in the amount of chemicals absorbed into their blood and vital organs.

During January, 2003, the Health and Safety Commission recommended that people who work with harmful dusts should not use nuisance dust masks to protect themselves from exposure because the masks were not considered adequate.

While a nuisance dust mask may prove futile in defending against poisons like Ricin as well as toxins like carbon monoxide and other chemicals and gases released by fires, it will reduce exposure to many other dangerous aggregates.

One thing is clear. Those with face masks will be better off than those without them. Extending that argument, a better quality face mask, such as those worn by painters to keep out toxic fumes, would offer greater protection. And those with a gas mask or oxygen mask would fare best of all. But the much-maligned nuisance dust mask might prove useful—and perhaps a lifesaver—in many situations. And it has the advantage of being inexpensive, small and lightweight. In fact, FEMA recommends that every family member have a nuisance dust mask with them at all times.

Dick Couch, author of the "Nuclear, Biological and Chemical Survival Manual" wrote, "If you are outside and a biological agent has been released (for example, sprayed from an airplane), seek immediate shelter inside a nearby building. If no shelter is available, attempt to get upwind of the agent. In any event, cover all exposed skin and protect your respiratory system as soon as possible." (Page 65). Captain Couch, of course, recommends complete military anti-chemical outfits. Lacking these, ordinary citizens need to provide themselves with the best protection available. A nuisance dust mask may not always do the job, but it in many cases it will be much better than nothing.

During the post 9/11 anthrax scares, postal workers were encouraged to wear inexpensive surgical face masks and disposable rubber gloves. Those items are available at discount and drug stores, home improvement warehouses, and warehouse clubs. During the winter of 2004-05, with its attendant shortage of vaccine, a few of the more prudent wore face masks and washed their hands frequently to avoid becoming contaminated.

Face masks are manufactured to meet the needs of various industries and professions. In spite of criticisms, most of them will offer some protection against smoke particles and biological threats like anthrax.

Warning: Nuisance dust masks will not protect from deadly fumes and toxins that may easily pass through their fabric.

In the event of a biological or gas attack, a gas mask or respirator with an air tank will, of course, be most desirable. But, for those of us on limited budgets—who are restricted by law from buying such devices—and who have limited space in which to store and carry such equipment, even a nuisance dust mask will offer some protection. Of course, the better the mask, the greater your chance of survival.

Surgical Face Masks

3M advertises that they are the industry leader in infection control face masks, and they advertise a complete line of filtration-efficient, fluid-resistant and comfortable-to-wear models to help reduce your exposure to potentially infectious particles.

The 3M™ ESPE™ surgical tie-on face mask, shown below, is soft, comfortable, fluid resistant, and adjustable to meet individual needs. It is easily folded to fit in your Pocket-Pack. It is so effective that it is advertised to stop the SARS virus as well as anthrax. The EXPE™ can be purchased in quantities of 50 for about fifty cents each. If carefully taped into position, it may be adjusted to fit even a small child or infants face.

3M SARs Resistant Surgical Face Mask

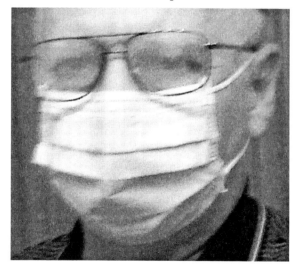

3M™ calls their ESPE™ Triple Layer Molded Face Mask the top of the line. It advertises "...exceptional fluid resistance..." and features a unique three-layer design that includes a fluid-resistant outer layer, a microfiber middle layer which "traps" microorganisms, and a soft, absorbent inner layer which absorbs moisture. This mask will take more space than a conventional tie-on face mask because the cloth mask can be folded, while this model has a molded shape. And while the ESPE™ Triple Layer Molded Face Mask is advertised for dental workers, it would appear to be applicable to emergency situations.

Surgical Masks in Cartons of 50

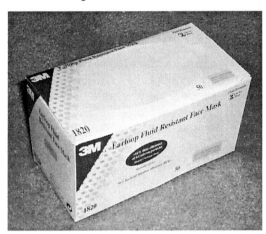

Surgical Gloves

Surgical gloves are vital for two reasons. If there is a chemical toxin or biological agent floating around, the gloves protect your hands. If you or someone to whom you are offering first aid has an infection, the mask and gloves will help keep the disease from being transmitted.

Caution: Be careful to avoid gloves made of latex rubber if there is any chance that you are allergic to latex. Look for a substitute. Some people actually go into shock and even die from close and prolonged contact with latex.

Surgical Gloves by Carton

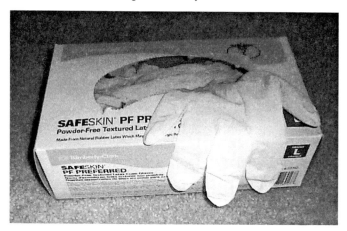

Goggles

If the need to escape from a fire—or if you are caught in the aftermath of an explosion—it is vital to protect your eyes from dust particles and chemical vapors.

Swimming Goggles

Swimming goggles were selected for this purpose because they are tough, they will keep biological agents, fluids, gasses and other blinding irritants from entering the eye, and they can be folding into a small package. The eye's surface is particularly susceptible to biological and chemical agents. Make certain that you try on your goggles and fit them comfortably to your own head before putting them in your Pocket Pack. You will not have the time once an emergency arises.

Swimming Goggles

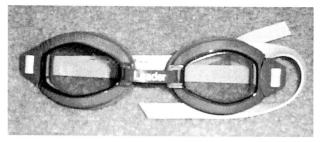

Safety Goggles

Individuals who requires eyeglasses will have to fit themselves with the larger safety goggles common to the woodworking shop. These goggles will fit over the glasses, but they will not prevent chemicals and smoke from reaching the eyes because they are loosely fitted and have vent holes. You should experiment with these to get the best and tightest fit.

Aluminum "Space" Blanket

Space Blanket

The Space Blanket pictured above is reported to be one of the fruits of NASA's vast labors. When folded, it makes a package approximately 2 inches by 3 inches, and less than one half inch thick. If you wrap it around a person, this compact and lightweight blanket retains an amazing amount of body heat, thus counteracting a major danger of shock. And, while this blanket will melt in an intense fire, it will reflect away a great amount of heat. If you have no alternative but to dash near or through some part of a fire, wrap it around yourself to improve your chances.

9. The Fannie Pack

Fannie Pack:
Weight, 12 to 16 ounces
Investment, $10 to $15

While everyone should carry the Pocket Pack described in the preceding chapter, its contents are limited. It's wise to carry an additional survival pack with more items.

The Fannie Pack is a significant upgrade from the Pocket Pack. While the Pocket-Pack can be carried in a pocket, backpack or purse, or hanging from a belt, the Fannie-Pack is carried around one's waist on its own belt.

If you plan to wear a Fannie Pack whenever you're away from home, don't carry a Pocket Pack. If you do decide to carry both, don't duplicate the items. Keep the three or four vital basics in the Pocket-Pack. If you need to carry more than one of any item, store the extras in the Fannie-Pack. The Fannie-Pack provides extra space to carry other items, such as a packet of fruit juice, a nutrition bar and even a small radio.

Fannie Pack

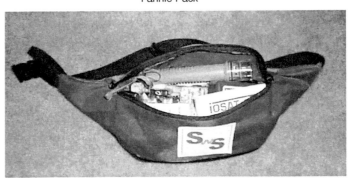

The extra items in the Fannie-Pack may help save your life. They may also save the life of a friend, neighbor, or loved one. And that person may in turn live to reciprocate your generosity by assisting someone else. This is the essence of survival with soul.

During a crisis many people rise above the quality of their everyday lives and often reveal themselves as heroic in character. When you make certain that you are equipped for every good work, you are not only preparing yourself, but you are also accumulating tools to help others. This sets you above the herd mentality and potentially makes you a hero. You won't be much of a hero, however, if you have to ask another poorly prepared person to share their limited resources with you.

While the Fannie-Pack contains more items than the Pocket Pack, it is still necessarily limited. The suggested contents speak for themselves.

- Compact First aid kit
- First aid tape
- Facial tissues
- Sanitary wipes
- Individually wrapped sanitary napkin, which can be used as a bandage
- Eye wash
- Latex exam gloves, which can also be used to protect one from biological contaminants
- Tylenol, ibuprofen or aspirin in a small package
- Disposable cigarette lighter
- Package of fruit juice
- Energy bar
- Package of potassium iodide tablets.

In addition to these items, you might fit a small flashlight into your Pack.

FANNIE PACKS

Available in most discount stores, Fannie Packs come in nylon, leather and many fabrics. Look for one that is durable, fits you comfortably, is large enough to be useful, and is sufficiently stylish.

FANNIE PACK CONTENTS

Always pack the basics for each person. Almost every individual has a special need.

Children require different items than adults. You should have potassium chloride tablets for the children. Older people become quickly dehydrated and also suffer from temperature changes. They require more fluids and must be kept warm.

Be careful of administering anti-depressants. In some cases, they are believed to result in suicidal or homicidal tendencies. Finally, you may need to dispense a certain medication, such as insulin or heart medicine. Remove less vital items in order to include what you require.

Fannie Pack Contents

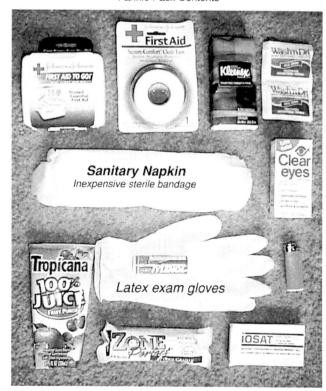

Potassium Iodide Tablets

Purchase potassium iodide tablets at your chain drugstore. Potassium Iodide is a non-prescription item, but you may have to order it at the prescription counter. You should have a 10 day supply on hand for each and every member of your family.

If you live within close proximity to a nuclear power plant, you may find that the government distributes these tablets free of charge. Check with your local emergency management people. This would save about $10 per person.

Potassium iodide should never be administered unless you are in imminent danger of exposure to radioactivity. It helps keep the thyroid from absorbing deadly radioactive isotopes that may have entered the bloodstream. It is more important to children than adults because their thyroids are more active. The drug will help prevent leukemia and other cancers.

Keep in mind that the entire body will be affected if you are exposed to the bombardment of radioactive particles. It is vital that you find shelter where there is at least a one-foot layer of concrete, or several feet of earth, separating you from the source of radiation. This means that, for fourteen days, you must hide beneath the earth, perhaps in a subway or in the center of a basement beneath a large masonry building of several floors. Hiding in a frame house will not protect you from the invisible and insidious radioactive rays. A dedicated fallout shelter is of course the best place to shelter if there is a nuclear incident.

First Aid Kit

During the Cuban Missile Crisis, a very fine physician emphatically stated that a typical home first aid kit would be a joke following a nuclear detonation. "You'll have to deal with more than splinters and minor cuts," he warned. "If you are injured at all, it will be a matter of severe burns, cuts, broken bones, concussions, internal injuries and even blindness. And that's not to speak of the mental trauma and depression associated with the deaths of those around you as well as the incredible change in your way of life."

First Aid Tape

A compact first aid kit generally contains only band-aids, a couple of pain killers, antibiotic salve, and similar products. Chances are, you'll need to treat larger wounds than the scratches children typically suffer during play time. Pack first aid tape so that you can secure a bandage. You may use any sterile pad for larger cuts, but we recommend that you include a carefully wrapped sanitary napkin for use as a heavy bandage. Learn to improvise. The Boy Scouts' *Manual* is an excellent source for emergency first aid, as is the American Red Cross First Aid Manual. For example, folded magazines or newspapers can be used as splints.

Facial Tissues

Facial tissues are useful for several purposes. Use them, of course, as handkerchiefs, but also to clean wounds and as toilet tissue.

Eye wash or eye drops

Even limited exposure to almost any kind of terrorist attack is likely to endanger the eyes. Dust and chemicals can irritate if not blind a person. Eye wash or eye drops will help in the treatment of less serious eye problems.

Latex exam gloves

Pack at least four latex exam gloves. Wear them to treat injuries or if there are possible biological agents in the area.

Sanitary Napkin

In addition to their normal use, these highly absorbent and sterile sanitary napkins are extremely useful as bandages. Carefully wrap them in clear plastic wrap to maintain their sterility.

Pain killers

Doctors recommend that you carry Tylenol to treat headaches and pain, ibuprofen for pain, inflammation and toothaches, and aspirin to treat heart attack and stroke. (Do not give aspirin to infants, children and pregnant women.)

Sanitary wipes

Use sanitary wipes to clean hands before touching your eyes, treating wounds, or eating.

Disposable cigarette lighter

Use a disposable lighter to signal people, to light the darkness, to start fires, and to ignite candles. Be careful of using candles in confined spaces. They are a frequent cause of fires, consume precious oxygen, and emit fumes that may be irritating or dangerous.)

Flashlight

Keep a flashlight to signal others, to find your way, prepare food, read and to light your life.

That One Cool Thing

First things, first! Make certain that you have the vital basics in your Fannie Pack. Then, if there is sufficient space, add one unique item that will make the most significant difference to you.

Though it may sound frivolous, nibbling on a chocolate bar might be just the thing to fortify both body and spirit during the dark hours of a long, cold night. Perhaps your teenager would be comforted with the diversion of a handheld computer game, while others would be enriched by the inclusion of a pocket New Testament.

Keep this in mind. When your world appears to be shattered, and when you or your loved ones are injured or ill, your core values rise to the surface. Things that seemed important prior to the crisis may now escape your attention. Concerns and relationships for which you have been too busy may suddenly become the most important things in the world. Carrying an old copy of *People* magazine so that you can catch up on the antics of Hollywood personalities at such a time may seem ridiculous. Your focus should be on spiritual reality and the best interests of friends and loved ones.

DON'T LOOK BACK!

You will pack the things that you consider important as you anticipate your needs for an emergency. The emergency itself will dictate your needs and alter your perspective. Should you face a situation in which you must rely on the items in your emergency pack, don't waste time ruminating over what you may have failed to include. Rejoice, instead, that you are among those who had both the foresight and conscientious spirit to prepare at all for such an emergency. Prayerfully make do with what you have. At all cost, do not criticize yourself or others.

Be positive. It's time to reinforce one another. Whatever things are good, pure, honest and true, always think on them.

10. The Day Pack

Day Pack and contents:
Weight, 5 to 10 pounds
Investment, $25 to $50

THE DAY PACK ITSELF

The Day Pack consists of a lightweight carrying container that would customarily be used in the kind of activities you engage. Depending on your occupation and interests, you might also choose a large pocket book, beach bag, attaché case, bowling ball bag, diaper bag, medical bag, salesperson's sample case, or laptop computer bag. In fact, the list is only limited by your imagination and the appropriateness of the container to your situation.

A backpack may the best overall choice for a comprehensive individual survival package because it is commonly used by students and travelers, is lightweight, has numerous pockets for separating contents, and is worn on your back, leaving your arms and hands free. It can be left in your car, either on the floor or in the trunk.

Lightweight, inexpensive Day Pack

DAY PACK CONTENTS

Bottle of Disinfectant

Every family member should carry a small bottle of household bleach. Use a drop or two to kill germs in a gallon of drinking water, or use a stronger solution to wash surfaces that may have become infected. The Family Pack, described in Chapter 10, should contain at least a gallon of household bleach.

Day Pack Content

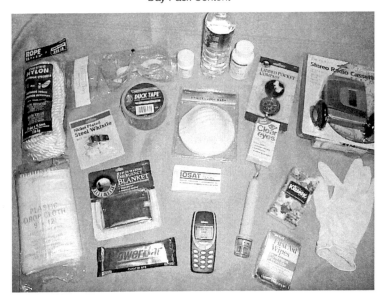

Portable Radio

The importance of a battery-powered radio cannot be over empha-sized. On 9/11, many people who were exiting the Twin Towers were told that it was safe to return to work. If they'd had access to portable radios, they might have been aware of the real dangers, and many more would have evacuated before the towers collapsed.

Flashlight

The importance of having a flashlight available in a building where the emergency lighting has failed or where smoke is a problem, cannot be overemphasized.

Water

We cannot live long without water, particularly when exposed to severe heat, or when in shock or dehydrated. In addition, water is vital for flushing eyes and wounds.

Non-prescription drugs

Aspirin, of course, is the medication of choice to combat heart attack and stroke, while ibuprofen and acetaminophen are administered to relieve inflammation and pain respectively, and antihistamines are used for allergic reactions. Small children may not be able to self-administer, but if the appropriate items are carefully packaged, a responsible adult may be able to assist your child. Important! Aspirin should not be adminis-tered to children or to pregnant women.

Prescription drugs

Even small children may sometimes have the training to self-adminis-ter their own insulin. If not, it will be necessary for a knowledgeable adult to manage this and other potentially dangerous drugs.

Nutrition bars

Nutrition bars may not be particularly attractive or palatable to a child, but when they become sufficiently hungry, they may prove a life-saver. What's more, they are very portable, so they can be carried in a pocket and eaten a bite at a time as desired.

50 feet length of nylon or poly rope

Rope has a multitude of possible uses. Tow a car out of traffic, pull a person from a swollen stream, or lower someone from a second floor window. It too is an item that should only be used under adult supervision.

When used to escape from an upper story, several ropes would offer an advantage. A number of individuals might have several ropes among them, making it possible to produce a makeshift rope ladder or a harness by which they could safely lower one another to the ground. It may be a surprise to many readers to learn that many small children have become familiar and comfortable with the use of ropes on rock climbing walls at school, in gyms and in shopping malls.

Pocket Bible

Some readers will feel that a Bible should not be included, while others will feel it should be the first item on the list. The fact remains that the scriptures contain the wisdom of the ages and can bring great comfort and encouragement to people in their darkest hours. "Thy word," King David wrote, "is a lamp unto my feet and a light unto my pathway."

Work gloves

A pair of gloves, either leather or cloth, may be worn over the more delicate surgical gloves to protect hands from biological agents, and hot or abrasive surfaces.

Writing Materials

A paper and pen or pencil will enable you to communicate with others, to leave notes for those you may miss at a rendezvous, to list important things that must be undertaken, or to set down your inner thoughts and increase your peace of mind.

Bandages

If you are caught up in a suicide bomb attack, it may require more than a band-aid to make repairs. A roll of gauze, first aid tape and bandages, including a triangular bandage, may be useful. The original Kotex type sanitary napkins are sterile and make excellent, inexpensive pads to cushion and stanch wounds.

It's vital that you stop any serious bleeding as quickly as possible. Your preparedness may mean the difference between life and death because emergency workers may not reach the scene for five or ten minutes.

Duct tape

Duct tape is useful for many things. FEMA recommends it as a means of sealing off an inner room in your house so that deadly chemicals and biological agents may be excluded for a short time. Once the oxygen is exhausted, you must have a tank of oxygen or compressed air available, or you will suffer asphyxia. You can purchase duct tape at your home improvement center in 2 inch wide, 60 yard long rolls.

Polyethylene sheeting

Polyethylene sheeting (9 mil), applied with duct tape, is also useful for sealing windows, doors and vent covers in a building in order to exclude chemical and biological agents. Hopefully these agents will be dispersed by the wind, they will break down, or the biological agent will complete its life cycle without infecting anyone. Stay in your safe room until you're sure.

Ski mask

Ski masks, as a rule, "breathe" too well to keep out chemical and biological contaminants. An excellent device for protecting much of the head would be a scuba diver's headgear. In fact, an entire wet suit would be very helpful. But any exposed skin will be a potential for contamination. Ski masks, on the other hand, are excellent for keeping warm.

Rubber bands (1/4" wide)

Use rubber bands to pull slacks up tightly around the socks at the ankle in order to keep biohazards from entering the pant leg. Pull the shirt sleeves in around the rubber gloves as well, using rubber bands.

SUPPLEMENTARY ITEMS

You may add other useful items, if family members are strong enough to carry them, such as extra food and water.

Israeli Gas Mask

The inexpensive Israeli gas mask, shown on the next page, protects against a number of chemical agents. It is infinitely superior to a nuisance dust mask in many ways and under numerous circumstances. Similar masks are available at military surplus stores and on the Internet. Shop around for the best buy. The filters are only good for a short period, so everyone has to have at least two of them. Such a mask is useless if it is not readily accessible when needed.

Gas Mask

WARNING: This particular gas mask is not adequate protection against all chemicals agents. And in situations where there is little or no oxygen available in the air, a mask with a re-breather or built in oxygen supply is required to prevent asphyxiation.

Because of a Few Bad Apples

As an aside, isn't it ironic that it is illegal for civilians to own gas masks with oxygen tanks because criminals use them to protect themselves while manufacturing illegal drugs? Isn't it remarkable that children are often prohibited from taking cell phones to school because a few bad apples use them to sell drugs? And isn't it annoying that many theaters and other public places are pressing to change the law so that they can install devices that will keep cell phones from working because they sometimes annoy people? Yet, the cell phone is the one device that may save the people in that place from terrorist attack. Once again, these are examples of the innocent suffering because of the rude behavior of a few.

Taser

If permitted by law, you may want to equip yourself with a Taser. The new consumer version Taser Stun Gun x26, with its USB charger, is available at the time of this writing at the Sharper Image.

If your life is in jeopardy, you may be able to subdue your assailant without seriously injuring him. Many people have used stun guns without just cause, and have seriously injured and even killed people with whom they were simply annoyed. By the time you read this, ownership and use of Tasers may be restricted by law.

Many missionaries use Tasers to save the lives of snake bite victims. If you point the Taser at the place where a snake or dangerous insect injected its venom, the high voltage shock will break down the complex proteins in both hematoxic and neurotoxic poisons.

Firearms

Where the law permits, adults who are properly licensed and trained may wish to carry a weapon. You may not, of course, carry a weapon on a commercial aircraft, but then you cannot carry a Swiss Army Knife or a corkscrew either.

DISGUISING YOUR SURVIVAL PACK

You can fit an extensive variety and quantity of survival items into a Day Pack. They will be useless however, if you don't have the pack with you when an emergency occurs.

If an emergency arises, your pack will suddenly become attractive to thieves who didn't have the foresight or wisdom to prepare one for themselves.

Since most people won't have any idea what you are carrying, you are not apt to be ridiculed for your preparedness. But any that ridicule you may later wish that they had made similar preparations. You may one day wind up saving their lives as well as your own. Remember, a mother looks perfectly normal if she's carrying what might be a large diaper bag. Business people look high tech when they carry an expensive laptop computer bag. A student is expected to carry a backpack. And a sun worshipper is expected to carry a large beach bag.

Does this mean that you have to have a survival kit to go with every outfit and occasion? Not at all. You can take your daypack and "diaper bag" to the beach. You can even put your "laptop bag" into the bottom of your beach bag so that it's beneath your towels and sun screen.

The right container will fit in with your occupation or activities, be easy to carry, sturdy, and relatively weather resistant. Above all, it must hold a variety of survival items. With a little practice, you can pack a lot of survival items in any container.

WHERE YOU CAN BUY THESE ITEMS

We purchased most of our items at major discount chain stores. The items are generally located in the following departments:

- Health and Beauty (Nuisance dust masks, aspirin, and related items)
- Pharmacy (Potassium Iodine, ibuprofen, hand sanitizers, first aid kits, eye wash, etc.)
- Sporting Goods (Flashlights, space blankets, water bottles, back packs, and more.)
- Home Improvement (Nuisance dust masks)

You can equip each member of your family with a pack that has everything on FEMA's check list for about twenty-five dollars.

Ready Made Backpacks Available

Incidentally, the cost of every device and survival item may initially rise if there is a nationwide enthusiasm on the part of responsible people to prepare themselves. But if enough Americans get on board, prices will drop because many more manufacturers and retailers will stock the items, and mass production and distribution will result in a lowering of the costs. Even now, chains like Walmart are offering equivalents to the Day Pack that contain survival items meeting FEMA's standards. Home Depot and Walmart have offered them for under $30.

STEP 4:

Prepare Emergency Food Supply

11. The Family Pack

Family Pack
2 weeks food and water per person
Weight, 125 to 200 pounds per person
Investment, $50 to $100 per person

SUPPLIES AND EQUIPMENT

Up to this point, we've been describing personal portable first response survival packs. These very small kits are designed to increase the likelihood of your survival in the midst of, or immediately following, a terrorist attack. They may also provide minimal food and water to keep you going for a day or two.

Now we turn to survival packs that are larger and less portable, packages that are designed for individuals, families and larger groups to promote survival over an extended period following a major attack or natural disaster.

These packages are properly stored in durable bins at home or the office, as well as in schools and other institutions. They contain the minimal items required to survive for a week or more.

There are a number of considerations in preparing a Family Pack.

HOW MUCH IS ENOUGH?

Determine How Long You Might Have to Wait For Help

First, decide how many days you might have to wait for emergency workers to locate you, to provide medical care, deliver food and water, set up shelters, and restore electricity and other vital services. Before you guess, think back over state and federal responses to other emergencies.

Keep in mind that terrorists want to make the situation as bad as possible. Tornadoes may be deadly, but they are mindless. They are just as likely to strike in the middle of a corn field as in the middle of a town. Terrorists, on the other hand, think carefully about where they will strike in order to cause the greatest harm. As a result, it might take a lot longer to receive assistance following a terror attack than it takes after a hurricane.

The Florida Experience

During 2004, Florida endured four hurricanes in seven weeks. At the end of that period there were still millions of people without electrical service, refrigeration, air-conditioning, and lights. They suffered shortages of gasoline, water, and ice. So, although you may consider a seven-day emergency food supply more than adequate, keep in mind that two full weeks after Hurricane Ivan struck Florida, some people were still living in public shelters. Worse, Hurricane Jeanne was about to strike. Months later, many people still did not have homes.

Although the State of Florida emergency personnel were assisted by FEMA, the National Guard, and other public and private agencies from all over America, many Floridians still lacked basic services. What's more, it was to be a long time before many could expect to occupy any kind of a residence following the destruction of their residences.

The Asian Tsunami Experience

Asian Tsunami Recovery

9.0 Quake 120,000+ Dead	Tsunamis Flood Coasts	Millions thirst, Disease threat	Nations begin pledging relief; USA sends two naval fleets	USA Reps Tour; Meet to Plan	U.N. to Lead Relief Efforts	After 2 Weeks, Millions in Need
Christmas, 2004	Dec 26, 2004	Dec 27, 2004	Dec 29, 2004—Jan 8, 2005	Jan 5, 2005	Jan 8, 2005	Jan 9, 2005

While we have had little experience with tsunamis in the United States, other major natural disasters regularly occur. It's instructional to recall how quickly the United States and other nations opened their hearts and their pocketbooks to assist the stricken southeast Asia nations. Yet, in spite of the speed with which aid was brought to the scene, there were still thousands who had not been assisted two weeks after the disaster.

Worse Case Scenarios

Imagine what the result would be if a conventional nuclear weapon were detonated in a major city of the United States. Hundreds of thousands might be dead, millions injured and ill. There would be chaos. Communications, transportation, food production, water and electrical supplies would be disrupted. Warehouses would be emptied. Food might not be available in some locations for a month or more!

If our government has to decide between diverting military vehicles to carry food and water to your area, or using those same vehicles to combat an enemy intent on destroying our way of life, their first responsibility will be to fight the aggressor. As in other lands throughout history, civilians would go hungry.

Minimum Requirements

Such an unhappy but not unrealistic scenario makes it clear that each of us should have a bare minimum of food and water on hand.

During the 1962 Cuban Missile Crisis, when nuclear war seemed imminent, we were advised to store at least a two-week supply of food and water. That arbitrary quantity would sustain us during the minimum estimated period that we would have to remain in a shelter in order to avoid the worst of the nuclear radiation.

Nowadays, with the danger of WMDs, you should not think in terms of less.

STORAGE ISSUES

Expiration Dates

Food products have different shelf lives. Most canned goods retain their flavor and remain safe to eat for one to three years. If a can is dented, or if there is any sign of leakage, you must discard it to avoid the danger of food poisoning. Some irradiated items, such as Twinkies, are said to have a fifty-year shelf life.

Date of Purchase

Always check expiration dates on the foods and beverages you purchase.

The retailers put the oldest products on the fronts of the shelves. You want the freshest items. So, check the dates as you put items in your cart.

In addition to checking the manufacturer's expiration date, you should print your date of purchase on every can, box and bottle with a black felt marker.

Make these items part of your regular meal plan. Use the oldest packages first. Then replace them during your weekly trip to the grocery store. The newest items are to be used last.

Labeling

In addition, cans and packages should be organized and labeled to make their contents easily identifiable. Finally, they should be repacked so that individual storage bins contain a cross-section of the most important survival items. This helps assure that, if cartons must be divided up among individuals because they may become separated, each carton will contain a variety of items necessary to their survival. Plastic storage bins that can be stacked are better than cardboard cartons because they are moisture and insect resistant.

Portability

No matter how well you organize your survival items, you should not simply stack them loose on shelves in your house or shelter because circumstances may arise that require rapid evacuation. Time may not permit you to gather, pack and load these items in your vehicle. Therefore these items should be stored in cardboard cartons, picnic coolers or plastic and metal storage bins to assure portability and to expedite emergency evacuation.

Storage Location

In order to extend the shelf life of your survival foods, you should take care not to store them in locations that are overly hot, cold, or damp, such as a cellar, unheated garage, or automobile trunk. Ideally, you will keep them in a relatively cool, dry place, away from insects, and safe from possible pilferage. Store them in a well-ventilated room from which items may be quickly moved to an automobile for evacuation purposes. Ideally, this room will be near the center of the house, without windows or an outside door. If you make one of your inside downstairs rooms into a "Safe Room," and you have sufficient space, it would be wise to store your food and emergency items there. The preparation of safe rooms and shelters is described later in this book.

Rotate Your Stock

You might opt for a twelve day emergency food and water supply.

If you do, try to pack each day's supply of food or water in a separate container. Label the front of each container with the name of a month, from January to December.

Each month, remove the contents of the box labeled with that date and mix it with your regular grocery items so that you use it up.

During your next trip to the grocery store, replace it's contents with fresh items and place the refilled container at the bottom of the pile. This way, you will be using up the oldest stock first and continually replenishing the stock with fresh food and water.

BE A CALCULATING INDIVIDUAL

Figuring out what you and your family may need to survive is easier than you think.

To some people, gathering and storing sufficient food and water may appear to be a daunting challenge, either too confusing or too costly. Yet, many people regularly stock a surprisingly large quantity of canned and packaged goods at home. And while the items you have on hand might not constitute the best balanced or most desirable diet, a quick inventory may reveal that you already have enough food on hand to meet your family's needs for a week or two. What's more, these foods are among your favorites.

Once you've listed the items you need for a two week period, it's only necessary to inventory what you have on hand so that you can calculate the additional items you will need to buy to round out your *Family Pack.*

This chapter offers a suggested list of items for your *Family Pack* including their estimated current costs.

Take the following steps to estimate how much it will cost and how long it may take you to assemble a *Family Pack.* You'll be surprised how quick and painless it can be to accumulate these items.

1. List the items you want in your personal or family survival pack.

2. Make a list of the items that you already have at home.

3. Subtract the items you already have from the total items you need to keep on hand. (For example, you plan to store two jars of spaghetti sauce. A quick inventory indicates that you already have one jar of spaghetti sauce in the pantry. Since you have one, but you want two, you need to buy one more. So you add one jar of spaghetti sauce to your Want List of things that you need to acquire.

4. Add up, or estimate, the total cost of the required items on your Want List.

BUDGETING

Determine how much money you think you can set aside each week to buy these items.Divide the estimated total cost of the items you need by the amount you can set aside each week.

This will reveal how many weeks it will take you to set aside sufficient funds to complete your Family Pack.

For example, if you believe that you need food and water that will cost a total of $250, but you already have food in your kitchen cabinets worth $100, then you only need to buy $150 more. Lets say that you can save $25 per week by careful management. Divide the additional $150 you need by the $25 you will set aside each week, and you can determine that it will take you only six weeks to complete your plan.

The exciting part is that you already have some things on hand, and you can add the most vital items starting the first week of your savings plan. With careful money management, and a little cooperation from family members in cutting back on special treats for a few weeks, you can complete your plan even faster.

Imagine that you only need a jar of peanut butter, a box of unsalted crackers, twelve gallons of water, and some dried fruit. You'd finish your plan in no time. Chances are, however, that your requirements will be much greater.

MAKING YOUR SELECTIONS

The Familiar and the Friendly

The choices that you make must balance your family's nutritional requirements with their individual tastes. That's always a challenge! It is best to serve them things that they enjoy and with which they are comfortable. Don't stock things that they have never eaten before, or that you know they don't like. Following an attack, everyone will be suffering emotional trauma. Avoid adding to the problem by trying to introduce an unfamiliar or unpalatable menu.

The tried and the True

What sorts of food should you include in your Family Pack? That should be pretty much dictated by what your family likes to eat. But even though a family member may love to eat one kind of food on a regular basis, it's possible that he may not care for it when under stress. You may discover that one or two have completely lost their appetites, while others have a compulsion to eat. Make certain that you store a variety of foods.

Stick to the tried and true and pray for the best. One man loves canned beef ravioli for breakfast. Well, it's obviously easy to store canned ravioli. He will be much easier to plan for than someone who insists on having scrambled eggs, bacon, home fries, buttered toast, and fresh coffee with sugar and half-and-half every morning.

Avoid Caffeinated and Alcoholic Beverages

Avoid foods that contain caffeine because people will already be over-stimulated. During the Cuban Missile Crisis, one doctor prescribed seda-tives in case someone were to become uncontrollable in the claustrophobic confines of a fallout shelter. Many people suffer emotional problems, and we may not discover them until we are in the middle of a crisis where we are unprepared to deal with them.

Try to satisfy your family's nutritional needs. Beverages may include canned or packaged fruit juices as well as powdered milk and hot chocolate mix for the children and instant coffee for the adults. Some will want soft drinks and alcoholic beverages, but alcohol is an unhealthy and even dan-gerous thing to introduce into an atmosphere of stress. Caffeinated bever-ages increase stress and stimulate appetites, and sugar tends to make children hyper.

Brighten up your days

Plan on four small meals a day, rather than three larger ones. They will help break up the boredom. Try to make them special. The English have their afternoon "Tea." Americans enjoy the morning "Coffee Break." Add something to your Family Pack that enables you to make a special presentation once a day, whether it consists of colorful napkins, elegant glassware, a floral centerpiece of artificial flowers, or a tablecloth. Brighten up your days. Try to break up the monotony and bring a little variety to your lives.

Beware unpleasant side effects

Let's face it. Most of us do not have the wherewithal to put charbroiled steak and baked potatoes on our survival menus. Meals may be comprised of freeze-dried foods that are manufactured for campers and back-packers, or canned and packaged foods right off your grocer's shelves. You may serve three people each a small portion from a can of stew or ravioli, then supplement it by dividing a can of vegetables, a few crackers, some canned fruit, and a cookie or cake.

You can vary the diet with canned tuna, chicken, Vienna franks, stew, spaghetti, franks and beans, and much more. You can also have trail mix and nutrition bars on hand for stacks. There are many great tasting prod-ucts on the market today. Beware of foods that result in indigestion or have other unpleasant side effects. You may be crowded together in a small room.

K.I.S.S.

Keep is simple, sweetie. Perhaps the simplest approach is to increase the stocks of things that your family regularly eats. Rotate your stock each month in order to assure freshness. Take some items out of your survival stores every week, then replenish them from the grocery store. Simply create a stockpile of your family's favorite foods. And, you will not have to add appreciably to your investment to increase the quantities that you keep on hand.

WANT LIST

Your Want List may look something like this. There is an additional copy of this form in Appendix A. Simply fill in the blanks.

Table 1: Suggested Foods for Storage

Items per package	Size, weight or volume	Description	Number needed	Less, number on hand	Equals, number to buy	Store price	Total cost
1	46 oz	Apple Juice				$1.59	
1	7 oz	Apricots, dried				$2.89	
1	15 oz	Baked beans				$.98	
7	1.2 oz	Breakfast Bars				$3.50	
1	Can	Potato chips				$1.40	
4	6 oz can	Tuna, canned				$1.40	
3	6 oz can	Chicken, canned				$1.50	
1	Can	Vegetable				$.89	
1	Carton	Cereal				$2.00	
1	Pint	Cheese spread				$1.98	
12	Pack	Cookies				$5.20	
1	Can	Chunky soup, canned				$1.99	
1	32 oz	Lemonade mix*				$2.99	
1	package	Rice, flavored				$.79	

4	bottles	Frappucino			$5.00	
1	15 oz	Fruit cocktail, canned			$.75	
12	12 oz	Ginger ale			$2.50	
1	46 oz	Grape juice			$2 .79	
1	Jar	Coffee, instant			$3.59	
2	Cups	Jello cups			$1.00	
8	package	Lance crackers			$1.84	
1	11.5 oz	Mixed nuts (unsalted)			$2.00	
1	package	Muffin mix*			$.71	
1	100 count	Multi-vitamin with Zinc			$5.00	
8	packages	Cereal bars			$3.44	
7	1.2 oz	Nutrition bar			$3.50	
1	46 oz	Orange juice, canned			$1.29	
1	15 oz	Peaches, canned			$1.09	
7	1.38 oz	Peanut butter crackers†			$1.75	
1	pint	Peanut Butter			$1.98	
1	46 oz	Pineapple juice, canned			$1.99	
6	12 oz	Powerade			$3.30	
2	cups	Pudding cups			$1.20	
12	individual	Oatmeal packets*			$3.39	
1	12 oz	Raisins			$2.49	

1	carton	Crackers, unsalted				$2.00	
1	15 oz	Soups*				$1.00	
1	16 oz	Spaghetti*				$$.79	
1	32 oz	Spaghetti sauce				$1.39	
1	15 oz	Ravioli				$1.59	
1	can	Spam				$1.59	
1	15 oz	Stew, chicken or beef				$1.95	
1	package	Stuffing mix*				$1.24	
1	4 lb.	Sugar				$1.40	
8	packs	Sugarless gum				$1.92	
10	packs	Hot chocolate mix*				$1.89	
48	bags	Tea				$2.99	
1	4 oz	Tuna or salmon pack				$2.10	
1	3.5 oz	Tuna salad				$1.19	
10	pack	Twinkies (or other)				$3.50	
1	46 oz	V8 juice (or other)				$1.89	
1	gallon	Spring Water				$.59	
1	carton	Wheat thins				$2.00	

SHOP IT AND STOCK IT

To recap, determine what you need. Make a list, round it out, add it up, and buy it.

Stack it all on a table, sort it logically, pack it in well-labeled boxes or plastic bins, and store it carefully. It's as simple as that!

SEPARATE IT, SACK IT, AND STACK IT

Stack all of these items in separate piles and then take one or two items from each pile and put them in one storage bin. Repeat the process until you've put away everything. Now you have a representative variety of items in each storage container.

Family Food Stockpile

Non-Food Items

You should also pack an inexpensive can opener, along with a quantity of plastic utensils, paper napkins, plates, cups and bowls in each container. If you should find yourself with only one storage unit, you will still have almost everything you need in one container.

It's wise to lay an inexpensive flash light at the very top of each container so that, regardless of the situation, you can shed a little light on the problem simply by opening a storage box.

In addition, to the canned goods, you can add packaged crackers and a half-dozen 16-ounce bottles of water. Many grocers and warehouse clubs sell individually-wrapped packages of crackers and cheese as well as assorted cookies in bulk.

Once a container is full, stuff some newspaper in to keep things from rolling about, snap down the lid, and apply a label that lists all contents. Tape over the label with clear packing tape to protect it from water damage.

First aid and medical items, extra clothes, and emergency supplies, such as portable radio, a compass, maps, extra eyeglasses and contact lenses, are packed in carefully labeled containers that will not be damaged by rough handling.

12. The Great Escape Pack

The Great Escape Pack contains items that should be stored in your automobile so that you are always prepared for unexpected emergencies.

Store your Great Escape Pack in your truck, SUV, or automobile

Whether you are ordered to evacuate the area within 30 minutes, or learn of an emergency while you are 30 miles from home, the Great Escape Pack contains at least a 3 day supply of food, water and emergency equipment.

Consider this scenario. You are at work and learn of an impending attack. You run out to your car and drive quickly to your children's school where you pick them up and head for home. But police direct your car to a highway leaving the city. Since you have your own food and water with you, as well as a two gallon can of fuel, you can leave the area without fear that your family will go hungry among the thousands of others who will be searching for food and shelter.

That's why everyone should have a Great Escape Pack. The Great Escape Pack consists of a cross section of the items that you have stored at home. It assures you that, even in a dire emergency, you have some of the items your family will require if you must evacuate the area.

STORAGE CONSIDERATIONS

Unfortunately, the trunk of a car and the back of an SUV are poor places to store food because vehicles are subject to broad temperature swings and variations in moisture. It is nonetheless vital that you store a minimum of survival items in your vehicle.

Packaging Methods

You may extend the useful life of the items you store in your vehicle by sealing them carefully in plastic bags or by wrapping them in foil and plastic and sealing them with tape. One way to protect clothing and first aid items is to compactly package them in the new plastic bags from which you evacuate the air using a vacuum cleaner, thus reducing their size as well as the air and moisture that might adversely affect them.

Keep the Weight Down

Limit the weight of individual bins. You don't want to risk injuring yourself trying to shift heavy boxes in a hurry.

Where to Store It

If your car is not likely to be broken into, it is a better place for storing many kinds of items than your house is. If you are away from home during an emergency, you will still have many necessities close at hand. If you are at home, chances are your car will be in the garage or at the curb and your items will be accessible. Here's the problem. If you have two cars, or if someone spends long hours at work and away from home, you have to decide in which vehicle to stash these items. Since the person at work may need them as much as the family at home, you may need to divide the items between home and car, or between home and two cars.

If you have four storage bins for four people, you might keep two at home and one in each vehicle. If you arrive home safely, you can carry a bin inside to shelter in place. If you need to evacuate, you can take the other two bins from the house to the car.

If you can afford to do so, you may simply wish to duplicate the items. If not, keep them in the car that is accessible to most family members, and is the vehicle that will definitely be used to drive to a rendezvous point as if required. Call this your primary emergency vehicle. You should store several kinds of items in the primary vehicle.

Make certain that the individuals who drive the second car carry fully equipped Fannie Packs with them at all times, and keep Day Packs in the car.

You already have day-to-day essentials and some emergency supplies in your home. You don't need to store your emergency evacuation supplies in the house. In fact, it is better to have them in your primary vehicle in case you need to evacuate quickly. It will be confusing enough to gather family members and last minute items. It's one less thing on your mind to know that your evacuation supplies are carefully packaged and stored in your escape vehicle.

What should you keep in the primary vehicle?

Store all evacuation items that will not be harmed by temperature and humidity in your primary vehicle. Store items that might be harmed by heat or cold somewhere in the house where you can quickly move them to the primary vehicle.

EXTRA ITEMS

Have a camping cook stove on hand so that, in the event that gas and electric are interrupted, you can still prepare hot drinks as well as soups and other canned foods. Remember that these camping stoves must be ventilated or else used outdoors, or you may asphyxiate yourself and your family.

Camping gear

Camping gear, while bulky, is useful in the event of an evacuation. Keep cooking gear, sleeping bags, ground cloths, and perhaps a compact lightweight tent in the vehicle.

Medical supplies

Medical supplies can also be stored in the car as long as the items won't freeze or be damaged by heat. This container should be well marked, and can be brought into the house if needed.

Sanitation and hygiene

Sanitation and hygiene items may also be stored in the car. These include facial and toilet tissues, disposable bags, soaps, and related items.

Water

Water, while heavy, should be among the first items packed. A gallon per person is minimal. That is less than a one-day supply. This water should be "rotated" out every few months to keep it fresh and potable.

Disposable kitchen items

Make certain that you pack paper plates, cups, plastic knives and forks, can openers, cooking utensils, and other disposables.

Clothing

You should also pack a change of clothing for each member of the family, putting them in tightly-sealed plastic bags and evacuating the air to make them compact. Clothing should include rugged play or work clothes, a sweater or a sweatshirt with hood, a windbreaker, knit hat, gloves, extra socks and underwear, and a rugged pair of walking shoes with waterproof soles. Equip each person with lightweight layers, so that they can be prepared for very warm or very cold weather.

Bedding and Sleeping Bags

Whether you go to a community shelter or sleep in your car, you will need sleeping bags or other bedding. Make certain that you pack waterproof sheets if you will be outside, as ground moisture will dampen your bedding and reduce its insulating quality. A roll of polyethylene builders plastic makes excellent ground cover and will also serve in constructing a wind breakers or a makeshift lean-too.

In cold weather, you can hang a space blanket six or eight feet from your campfire to reflect the heat back at you.

Dehydrated Foods

A portion of your food supply might include dehydrated meals, packaged trail mix, energy bars, and dried fruit and nuts.

Tool kits

Don't forget some simple tools in case you have to camp out or make car repairs. A hatchet, a folding shovel, a small tool box containing assorted screw drivers, pliers, wrenches, a hammer, etc., should be packed in an easily accessible place.

Emergency Equipment

You should have a medium sized ABC fire extinguisher in the front of the car as well as a first aid kit. Many families have lost their cars or RVs because they haven't had the means to put out a small fire.

How Much Stuff Can You Carry?

If evacuation is mandated, and you have the opportunity, load additional storage boxes from your home survival package into your vehicle before leaving. Make certain that you leave adequate room in your vehicle for your most precious trust, your family. Make certain each one is well protected in a safety seat if mandated by law. Don't overload your vehicle! You are more subject to rollovers because of the added weigh. Remember, you may be forced to make drastic maneuvers on highways populated by panicked drivers. Keep heavier cartons, such as canned goods, near the floor and positioned between the axles. Put lighter articles, like sleeping bags, at the top of the pile and in the rear behind the axle.

How Many Evacuation Vehicles?

If you own more than one car, you must decide whether to take one or both of them during the evacuation. Take two cars if it does not increase the likelihood of your being separated and unable to protect one another. Otherwise, take the most reliable, high-mileage vehicle that will carry supplies as well as family. If you've established firm places of rendezvous, if you have sufficient fuel in both cars, if you have two competent drivers, and if you plan to be careful to stay together, taking two cars will enable you to carry more supplies and people, and provide backup transportation in the event of a breakdown.

At this point, your car is probably overly full and you have no space left to use it for the regular chores, such as bringing home the weekly groceries or car-pooling the soccer team. Try to balance the items that you want to store in your primary evacuation vehicle against your regular needs for this vehicle.

Before You Run for It...Turn Off Utilities

In the event of a major disaster-such as a tornado, earthquake, hurricane, or nuclear incident, be prepared to turn off the utilities to your home. A break in a gas or electrical line could result in an explosion or fire that could destroy your home and its contents.

Familiarize yourself with the location of your electrical circuit box, gas meter and water supply valve. These may be on the outside of your house, in a utility room, in your garage, or basement.

If you are to remain at home after an attack has occurred, you may want to leave the utilities turned on. But if the threatened attack has not occurred, turn them off. If you are preparing to evacuate your home, and you have sufficient time, turn them off.

Shut Off Electricity

Caution: Make certain that you are not standing in water when you attempt to disconnect electricity.

Circuit Breakers

If you have a breaker box, open the door, then snap the levers on the main breakers to shut off the power. They are generally located at the top of the box, above the parallel rows of smaller breakers. If in doubt, shut off all the circuit breaker switches.

Typical Circuit Breaker Panel

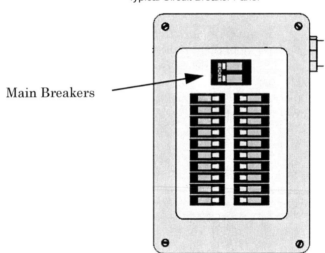

Main Breakers

Fuse Panel

If you have an older fuse panel, grab the handle on the main fuse block and pull it straight out of the box as shown on the following page.

Typical Fuse Panel

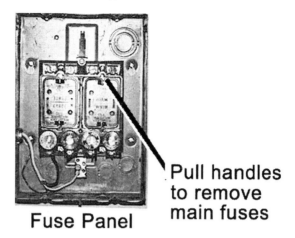

Fuse Panel

**Pull handles
to remove
main fuses**

Shut Off Gas

Locate the shut-off valve on the pipe leading into the gas meter. This is probably located along the side of your home. Buy a wrench to fit the valve, then chain or wire it to the pipe so that it is available to quickly turn off the gas. To turn off the gas, turn the valve 1/4 turn, or 90 degrees, so that the valve runs perpendicular across the pipe.

Drawing of Typical Gas Valve

Gas pipe

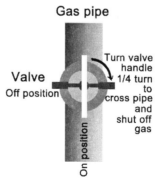

Valve
Off position

Turn valve
handle
1/4 turn
to
cross pipe
and
shut off
gas

On position

Shut Off Water

Shut off the valve from the municipal water supply or from your well. This will prevent large quantities of water from flooding your home if a pipe is cracked or broken. If you have a municipal water supply, the valve may be next to the meter in a below-ground housing at front of your house, near the curb.

If you have a well and pump, there should be a valve at the pump, as well as at the pressure tank. Turn off the valve leading into the pressure tank as well as the valve between the pressure tank and the house. Otherwise, an additional twenty gallons or more of water will be under pressure and ready to leak out of your pipes. Since you've already turned off the electric, your well pump will not continue to operate.

Close and Lock Doors and Windows

If time permits, shut and lock all windows and doors before leaving the house.

WHEN YOU RETURN HOME

You may not be permitted to return to your home until authorities have checked it out. If you are, make certain to follow these procedures.

Do not immediately turn the utilities on. Check to see whether the house has been damaged.

Make certain that there is no odor of leaking gas. If there is, don't turn on the electricity and don't permit an open flame. It could set off an explosion that would destroy the house and kill or injure you. Instead, open the windows and doors to ventilate the house. Then determine the source of the gas. Be careful of entering the basement if there is a gas leak. Gas is heavy. It will fill the basement first. You may be asphyxiated.

Turn the water back on and check for leaks before restarting the water heater.

Before turning power back on, make certain that your air conditioner and refrigerator are turned off. After you reset the breakers or reinstall the fuses, turn them on one at a time. They draw a great deal of power.

If there is no gas odor, reset the circuit breakers or reinsert the fuse block. If local power has not been interrupted, your lights should go on. Now turn the refrigerator and heating or cooling system back on.

Turn on the gas. Immediately check the pilot lights on water heater and kitchen range to make certain they are lit. Otherwise, you'll have a slow gas leak into the house.

STEP 5:

Promote Preparedness

13. Corporate & Institutional Packs

CORPORATE DISASTER RECOVERY AND PLANNING

Disaster Recovery and Planning generally describes the preparations for, and planned responses to, an emergency that endangers the information technology assets of an organization. A single corporation's data may represent the labors of tens of thousands of highly-trained people over many years. In some cases, this information can represent hundreds of millions of dollars.

This definition, however, is too limited.

How Employees are Viewed by Many Executives

People are ultimately at the heart of every enterprise, either as customers, clients, partners, executives, managers, or employees. Yet, many executives consider information to be a far more valuable asset than the employees who create it.

They believe that they can replace their "human resources" more easily than they can replace technology and information. That argument notwithstanding, if corporate owners don't have people at some point in the enterprise, the information has little purpose. As a rule, if a profitable enterprise requires few employees, they are generally more valuable and very difficult to replace.

When corporate employees sense that management doesn't care about protecting them, they come to care less about working for that company. This isn't supposition. The labor movement grew out of a sense that labor was being exploited by management. That same feeling is now arising among white collar workers.

How do employees retaliate against an indifferent or distinctly exploitative management? They cease to be productive and creative, they look elsewhere for opportunities, and they encourage those around them to do likewise. Their revenge is to stifle the growth of the company that they perceive is mistreating them. This is the free market economy in action.

If management doesn't look out for the best interests of its employees, a competitor who is perceived as a better employer will hire them away. Or a vendor. Or a client.

Some corporations may not want to spend money to protect their employees, but do so because it's prudent. Personnel retention has become a vital concern of modern enterprise. It costs a lot more to recruit, orient and train new employees than it does to retain existing ones.

What goes around really does come around. "No man is an island." Businesses do not operate in a vacuum. They must be perceived as taking care of their employees or they will lose them!

Around the year 2000, a conscientious employee wrote a recommendation to the president of a smaller technology company in San Diego, suggesting that they should prepare for a terrorist attack or other natural disaster that could (1) interrupt services, (2) destroy enterprise assets, and, far more importantly, (3) harm employees. The suggestions were offered in good spirit, but were at first ignored, then openly treated with contempt by executives. No direct response was ever offered.

The Value of the Employee

Employees are a business's most precious resource. They are often also consumers and stockholders. When a company establishes a human resources department, it is equating human beings with mere office equipment and carpeting. Yet when a company damages a file cabinet, it can replace it for a couple of hundred dollars. When a company loses people, it loses the repository of knowledge, skill, dedication, and commitment required for ongoing success in achieving the organization's mission. The business becomes an empty shell consisting of non-human resources that are useless without humans to manage or make use of them.

Many of us have achieved something above and beyond the call, and then have had a manager ask, "That was yesterday; what are you doing for me today?

Well, let's put the shoe on the other foot. The information technology that corporations spend a fortune to archive and protect was also created yesterday. Much of it is instantly out of date. Yet, corporations spend a fortune to protect it. Employers should ask, "Who's going to make yesterday's technology work tomorrow? Who's going to come up with the new technology that moves the business ahead?" Not ex-employees.

On 9/11, we lost thousands of America's finest business people. Hundreds of stockbrokers and financial experts lost their lives in the Twin Towers. At least one entire company was so devastated by the deaths of employees, including executives, that it virtually disappeared. Perhaps some employers would consider these people to be easily replaced human resources, but to their families, their company, and to America, they are now remembered as precious human beings, not commodities.

How Employees Often View Executives

In the past, employees looked with favor on companies that offered benefits like health care, extended vacations and profit sharing plans. Now employees are beginning to look with favor at companies that take measures to provide for their health and safety. Employees have shown their concern for security by moving from the cities to the suburbs, and from the suburbs to the countryside. Some pay exorbitant amounts to do so. They commute many hours each day. As much as is convenient, they avoid tall buildings, airplanes, and crowded public places. Some have put the 9/11 terrorist attacks out of their minds, but if there is another successful attack, we will be forcefully shaken out of our malaise.

THE NEW DISASTER AND RECOVERY APPROACH

It costs a great deal for a company to protect its information assets. But it really isn't that expensive for a business to provide fundamental protection for employees. It may cost the stockholders a few bucks per employee, but the corporate bottom line may improve as a result of these actions. And if there is another disastrous attack, some companies may find themselves a lot better off than competitors who failed to take steps to protect their staffs. By protecting their people, companies will be able to keep on churning out products and services. Consider these advantages of preparation:

First, businesses will earn valuable goodwill from their employees. Second, they may actually help keep their employees alive and well, and their equipment functioning effectively. They may avoid the downtime experienced by their competitors and actually be able to exploit the situation.

This chapter discusses some of the inexpensive steps that companies can take to protect their employees, and, as it happens, their own best interests. If executives look closely enough, they will realize that they too are employees of their corporations and they too are subject to the same dangers that a terrorist attack, an earthquake, or a hurricane represents to everyone else in the plant. Of course, they can vote themselves benefits that their employees don't enjoy. But word will get around, and employees will resent the disparity.

NATIONAL EMERGENCIES AND CORPORATE POLICY

In the event of major protracted struggles like World War II, governments actually require citizens to take certain steps to protect life and property. But this isn't World War II. So, your preparations are voluntary.

War as We Knew It

Some of our seasoned citizens remember the pails of sand, painted red, with letters picked out in white that spelled "Fire." Those buckets reposed next to dusty acid-foam fire extinguishers in shops, warehouses and factories during World War II. Federal law required the presence of those buckets because, in the event that an enemy airplane dropped incendiaries, the sand could be used to smother the otherwise unquenchable and intensely hot firebombs. Early in the war, Air Raid Wardens were appointed to enforce restrictions that required that people "black out" their homes and offices at night. Windows were covered with opaque curtains so that the crews of enemy aircraft could not see the lights from high above. As World War II wound down, and the threat of invasion in the United States became less of a concern, some of these restrictions were relaxed. Today, blackouts are irrelevant because missiles use global positioning systems to find their targets.

A New Kind of War

This is a different age. Different precautions are required to limit the impact of a small group of fanatical terrorists intent on using WMDs. A bucket of sand won't do much good against a home-made dirty bomb.

Yet, in spite of numerous warnings by top governmental agencies and the military, we have not been put on a wartime footing to mandate any civilian preparedness. In contrast, Israel issues gas masks and requires the storage of food, water and other emergency supplies. Such policies here might rattle the population and stagger the economy.

Few Americans have experienced the horror of a terrorist attack, and God helping us, they will not. But, for those of us who will examine the evidence, terrorism represents a real and present danger.

The Bottom Line

Corporate executives feel that their first responsibility is to their stockholders. They hate to spend money on anything like fire extinguishers or sprinkler systems, and do so only because it is required by law and because it keeps insurance premiums down. That's why insurance companies and local fire inspectors regularly check equipment to make certain that it meets requirements. Many executives consider such measures to be a cost of doing business, while insurance companies consider them a means of reducing their liability, and fire personnel recognize that they limit potential damage. If a fire strikes, executives are delighted that they had these measures in place. But, until they are needed, fire extinguishers are much like insurance, or preparations for terrorism—a necessary evil.

Conditions are now different because we know that an enemy who is armed, able, and dedicated is intent upon doing us a great deal of harm.

Corporate Vulnerability

In the case of most companies, the idea that a terrorist might directly attack is a fantastic idea, remote and absurd. It's more reasonable to assume that the terrorists will save their efforts for a major industrial facility, like an oil refinery or a nuclear power plant. Such an attack could harm thousands or even millions of people and destabilize our economy. And they may be right. Employers need to realize, however, that a major attack will result in the interruption of communications, transportation, electricity, and fuel, and perhaps cause much greater harm.

When the Twin Towers collapsed, a cloud of unhealthy dust spread over much of Manhattan. But, people as little as fifty miles away might have remained completely ignorant of the disaster for quite some time had it not been for two things. The collapse of the towers was displayed on national television, and the destruction of this major center of communications resulted in the interruption of Internet and telephone services as well as stock market operations. And the trauma produced by this attack had near catastrophic results for our national spirit as well as on an economy that had already begun to sink into recession during the end of Clinton presidency.

What employers fail to understand is that an event might occur that seems remote, but that would have catastrophic consequences for their companies and employees.

Nearby Targets

That little technology company that ignored the suggestion that they prepare was situated in San Diego County. With a population of over 3-million people, the county covers over 10,000 square miles.

San Diego is a prime target for terror. Virtually all of the potable water flows into the county through canals hundreds of miles long. The nearest significant power generation facility is the often criticized nuclear power plant at San Onofre, twenty miles north, on the Pacific coast. The south end of the county forms the border with Mexico, where illegal aliens and terrorists are able to sneak across each day. San Diego itself is home to several of our aircraft carriers, as well as major marine and navy bases. (In

1941, the Japanese attacked Pearl Harbor hoping to destroy the three air-craft carriers of our Pacific Fleet. We evidently have still not learned that we should not put all of our eggs in one basket.)

Consider, for example, the attacks that have been made on our troops and the people of Iraq by foreign terrorists. No deadly attack has been too small! They did not hesitate to detonate a bomb along a Bagdad street that resulted in the death of innocent school children.

The purpose of terror is to terrorize, and nothing so effectively accomplishes that end as to harm a dozen people in some remote location such as a small business or a local post office. Most people would conclude, "If they can blow up people in that little place, they can blow up people in my little place." Even if you leave the big city and dwell in a small village, you realize that you can no longer feel safe. With that realization, fear is born and anxiety mounts. We all come to fear a direct attack upon us in the places we live or work or play.

Through early 2005, the Bush administration had succeeded in preventing a second attack. Since the terrorists were preoccupied with the middle East, and since they are being forced to keep their heads down in the United States, the possibility of such small and isolated attacks currently seems remote.

Remote or not, every employer has both the privilege and responsibility to help you survive. They need you to build and maintain their business. Hopefully they will need you in the future. Just as they provide rest rooms and a snack area for employee comfort, and install fire extinguishers and surveillance camera to protect their investments, so they should invest a reasonable sum in facilities, supplies and equipment to preserve employee's lives.

In most cases, the executives are also employees. It is a cruel trick if the corporation provides special facilities to protect executives while leaving other employees to rely on their own devices. But if they do, then the employees should act to protect themselves by assembling the personal survival packs described in this book.

SCENARIOS

What Happens If There's a Biological Attack?

What happens if you are at work and you learn that there has been a biological attack? Thousands could be dying, and government emergency management personnel could order people to remain where they are until further notice.

What happens if highways in and out of your city are closed in order to prevent a spread of the contagion, your spouse is miles away at his or her workplace, and your children are locked down in their schools or are home alone, and you are not allowed to leave your work place? Will you, and they, have the supplies and equipment that are required in order to survive?

Your Worst Nightmare

What happens when the power goes off, when the heat or air-conditioning shuts down, and when the water pressure drops? If the water supply is restricted, the water sprinkler system will not be effective for fighting fires. If the electricity goes off, computers will shut down, servers and hard drives will come to a grinding halt, and the occasional standby generator will start up to supply the computers.

You may not be able to reach your loved ones by phone because communications have been interrupted or because terrified people are flooding the system with calls.

Employees will wander around their buildings until the batteries on the emergency lighting systems run down. Then they will stumble about in the dark, trying to learn what is happening, hoping to find someone with a battery powered radio.

They'll go to the fountain for a drink, but there may be no water. Toilets may not flush, and bathrooms may smell. There will be no doughnuts left in the lunch room and the vending machines will be empty. Authorities may require them to remain in the building for at least 72 hours, and emergency workers may be too busy with the dead and the dying to be concerned or able to bring food, water or blankets to the building.

Terrorism Isn't the Only Danger

Earthquakes, hurricanes, tornadoes, tsunamis, floods, and ice storms can all disrupt the life of a community and a business. Preparation is prudent.

Recently, a power plant at a refinery near Houston blew up and produced an uncontrollable blaze. People throughout the area were told to remain indoors, shut their windows and doors, and turn off air conditioning systems. The hydrocarbons in the atmosphere made it more dangerous to evacuate than to remain inside an enclosed structure. Fortunately this occurred at night when people were at home with their families, and in springtime when the cooler weather meant that the homes would not become unbearably hot.

AN OUNCE OF PREVENTION...

Corporate disaster programs should look more to prevention, not simply in terms of Internet security and industrial espionage, but in terms of preparing and responding to terrorism and natural disasters. The wisest companies will promote the best interests of their employees as well protect their facilities and their intellectual property. As a result, they will gain a significant edge over those competitors who are not prepared for any form of attack or natural disaster.

There is no question that employees will experience anxiety if they are locked down in the workplace. That could occur because the air outside is dangerous to breathe, because the highways are gridlocked or must be kept open for emergency and military personnel. Even if the lights remain on, they may be in the dark concerning the locations and welfare of their loved ones.

There will be little in the way of medical supplies. In fact, employers are reluctant to hand out so much as an aspirin because of the fear of lawsuits. Yet, that very aspirin might save the life of an executive who is at risk for heart attack or stroke. Likewise, a defibrillator might be priceless, as would employees trained in emergency first aid and CPR.

A home improvement store that sells caustic liquids may be forced to provide an eye washing system under insurance company guidelines. They may have to post emergency phone numbers and keep trained personnel on staff. But the typical employer will not be able to offer a Tylenol, let alone have people on hand trained in emergency medical procedures, such as the Heimlich Maneuver or cardio pulmonary resuscitation. Ironic, isn't it?

WHAT'S A BODY TO DO?

So, what does a company do for its people? It's not really necessary that the company spend a lot of money on supplies and equipment. They might pay a volunteer to conduct a few brief meetings to advise employees how they can protect themselves. They might encourage each employee to bring in a small supply of food, water, and a battery-powered radio. They might put up posters, run promotions through their employee newsletter, and even provide time for training sessions. They could even suggest that employees keep an extra sweater or a folded blanket in a spare file drawer or a locker.

What Steps Should Management Take?

Management shouldn't simply set up processes to protect computers and data. Management should prepare to help save its the lives of its employees. At a minimum, they should consider setting aside some emergency supplies, if only cases of bottled water. And they can arrange for some of their people to receive emergency medical training. In the midst of this long-term national emergency, real corporate leaders can demonstrates that they care about their employees and that they are trying to protect the entire team. Corporations need to establish a planning committee, with a real budget and real deadlines, to establish a meaningful program.

THE CORPORATE PACK

Every corporation needs a "Corporate Pack." This might be comprised of pallets of supplies, shrink-wrapped, and safely tucked away in a clean, dry store room where they can only be accessed by authorized personnel. Items might include a three day supply of water for each employee (three gallons per employee), energy bars, trail mix, or packaged foods sufficient to last a couple of days, medical supplies, emergency flash lights, battery-powered radios, a few walkie-talkies (to communicate around the facility), perhaps and an emergency generator and fuel.

Every prudent employee will keep an individual survival pack in a desk drawer or a locker. This should include at least two 2-liter bottles of water. This will help them survive whether there is an immediate problem in their work area or they have to evacuate the building. Your own preparation is an absolute necessity if you work for an otherwise conscientious, but under-financed, employer.

Water

Every employer should store at least three gallons of water per employee, and should arrange to change it out for fresh water at least once a year. They can buy water for as little as 25-cents a gallon. If you are locked down in a building for a full day, with both water and electricity cut off, you will need a minimum of the one gallon of water, particularly if it is summer and the building becomes oppressively hot. You could suffer heat prostration or stroke.

If the company has a water tank or water tower of substantial capacity, arrangements should be made to disconnect it from the public water supply if that supply becomes contaminated or suffers pressure loss. Water should be rationed. If the facility is located in a rural area, and has its own well water supply, the continued flow of water could be better assured with the installation of an electrical generator.

If the company may has a large water heater on premises, it too may be disconnected from the system and the water reserved for hygienic or drinking purposes. Turn off the gas or electric to the water heater(s) if the water supply is terminated.

Where water is available, but may contain bacteria, add a drop or two of household bleach to each gallon of water. Then allow it to set for an hour.

Use counter top filter systems to produce a better tasting product.

Stimulants, such as coffee and tea, may be useful in treating shock, and would be an excellent addition to the Corporate Pack. Their use should be limited because they can upset already nervous people.

Food

You should enough food on hand to last a couple of days. Include at least one low-sugar nutrition bar or some trail mix and dried fruit. Keep the salt level down so that you it doesn't increase problems with thirst.

Power

Every company ought to have a standby generator that automatically starts producing power the instant the commercial source of electricity falters. This generator should power the computer hardware for at least a few hours. In addition, it should have sufficient fuel and adequate duty cycle to run emergency lighting as well as equipment for heating soups and hot drinks.

Counselor

It might be possible to have provide training to a staff member willing to volunteer to counsel emotionally troubled people during an emergency.

STEP 6,

Provide for Shelter

14. Safe Rooms and Shelters

WHY SHELTERS?

An Ageless Need

We all believe in shelters. Much of the history of the human race involves the development of shelters to protect us from the elements and from predators—both two and four-footed.

Our homes are actually very sophisticated shelters. So are our offices, factories, schools and shopping malls. They are designed to let in light, clean air, and fresh water, while exhausting unhealthy air and waste water, and continually maintaining the temperature and even the humidity with precision. Even our automobiles and airliners are forms of shelter that coddle while conveying us.

We must have shelters for several very obvious reasons. Our homes are places of retreat, of privacy, of safety, of comfort, and, hopefully, of love. We must have shelters to keep us warm, dry, clean and healthy. We must have places to store, prepare and eat our food. We must have shelters to rest and recreate. And we must have them to protect and preserve our hard-earned possessions.

Kings live in palaces, the very wealthy live in mansions, Troglodytes dwell in caves, some live on boats or in RVs, but most of us live in houses, apartments and condominiums. And while we like to make them as stylish and comfortable as we can, their basic function is to shelter us.

As a nation, we confidently store our money in banks because they shelter it from thieves, fire and other depredations, or we invest it in diverse enterprises that shelter it while returning some measure of security and profit. We design our distribution systems so that our food supplies are efficiently stored in warehouses, refrigerated trucks and grocery stores. We have a very complicated and fragile infrastructure that has developed numerous kinds of shelters for many purposes.

Americans and Shelters

Over the past three centuries, many Americans dug root cellars in their back yards that also served as tornado shelters. Some of our pioneer forefathers dug small cellars beneath the floors of their cabins to hide from their enemies. Others built blockhouses to safeguard their families. During the War Between the States, those who supported the "Underground Railway" had secret rooms built in or near their homes in which they hid runaway slaves, while others in the south dug tunnels from their cellars so that they could escape outlaws and raiders. During World War II, Corey Ten Boom—the Dutch Christian who helped save thousands from Nazi death chambers—had a tiny room cunningly designed for secreting Jews until she could move them on to safety.

SHELTERS IN TIME OF WAR

The Cold War and the Fallout Shelter

Throughout the ages, the human race has had to contend with earthquakes, pestilence, tornadoes, tsunamis, hurricanes, plagues, and, always, warfare.

During the Cuban Missile Crisis of 1962, a large but unknown number of Americans built fallout shelters in their back yards or cellars. Nowadays, tens of thousands more are building safe rooms and panic rooms within their homes.

During the Cold War, the U.S. government printed millions of pamphlets encouraging and instructing Americans how to build back yard and basement fallout shelters. These shelters were not designed to protect from the blast and heat of a nuclear explosion, but from the resulting clouds of nuclear fallout and its deadly radiation.

The government was criticized for some of these designs on the ground that they might be dangerous. The "Better Red Than Dead" crowd, the leftist network news commentators, and the one-worlders in Congress criticized the entire Civil Defense effort. Their motives notwithstanding, their words influenced international politics and kept us on military parity with the Soviet Union until Ronald Reagan ended the Cold War. Those folks are still around today, trying to get us to submit our nation to world opinion and to the control of the United Nations, and, as always, seeking to appease our enemies, both foreign and domestic.

They discouraged the construction of fallout shelters then, and they discourage the construction of safe rooms now. Common sense dictates, however, that we do build shelters, just as the English were forced to do during World War II,

In foreground, John Becker, with brother Bill, preparing the shelter foundation in Staatsburg, New York, 1962. The tunnel to the house basement is in the center of the photograph.

One of the government's inexpensive shelter designs called for the construction of a basement shelter. It was to have a plank roof about a foot below the existing basement ceiling, with several layers of solid 4"-inch concrete blocks between them to shield the survivors below from deadly radiation. But the critics argued that if the house were to burn down, the shelter's occupants would be asphyxiated or burned to death. What the critics ignored was the fact that the house was unlikely to burn down unless subject to the actual blast of the bomb. And if it was exposed to the actual blast, the occupants would die anyway. But without the shelter, the residents would surely die from radiation poisoning whether the house burned down or not.

Shelters as a Defense Against Weapons of Terror

Terrorists are seeking access to weapons of mass destruction. Depending upon what kind of weapons they are able to secure, the nature of their attacks will vary from suicide bombers that kill a few victims at a time to highly-trained, well-supported groups using weapons of mass destruction to murder millions.

In times past, society's outlaws expressed their evil in various ways. We still have our serial killers, rapists, child-abusers, gang members, drive-by shooters, drug dealers, those who exhibit road rage, and many more. Now we have to add organized terrorists to the list.

We've already experienced our Timothy McVeigh and Terry Nichols who, working pretty much alone, bombed a federal government building. Now we must try to contain tens of thousands of misguided fanatics who have joined a cause to kill freedom-loving people and who will bring down civilization around their own ears. Those terrorists who come from relatively primitive Third World societies cannot imagine how the destruction of civilization will harm them. But, if and when hordes of savage warlords begin sweeping across their lands, stealing their pitiful possessions, razing their homes, raping their women, making slaves of their children, and butchering them in their own turn, they may tardily realize that the civilization they tried to destroy had brought some semblance of peace and security even to their isolated little worlds.

People around the world have discovered that terrorists can indeed shock an entire nation, and nearly bring down its economy, simply by setting off a few bombs or crashing a few jetliners. The 2004 train bombings in Spain were used to blackmail the people of that country into electing officials who were willing to appease Al Queda by pulling Spain's troops out of Iraq. Just as the appeasement of Hitler by Britain's Neville Chamberlain invited additional depredations, so any appeasement of terrorism encourages that bully down the block to increase his bullying. As a result, we are faced with what could be many years of terrorist activity.

Shelters As Deterrents to War

Had we put America's civil defense effort on a sufficiently high plane during the 1960s, it would have acted as a deterrent to Soviet aggression.

Shelters were the civilian's last best hope for survival if and when diplomacy failed. Today, we cannot rely on diplomacy. Our former allies seek to appease terrorists, while the terrorists have only one unremitting goal, to destroy us.

If enough Americans prepare themselves with emergency training, survival equipment, places of shelter, and an attitude of faith, they will constitute a powerful deterrent to terrorist attacks. When would-be assassins see that the sacrifice of their own lives achieves less "success" in terms of people injured or killed, they will be more hesitant to make that sacrifice.

To sum up, in time of war—and this is a time of war—we need special shelters to protect us from weapons of mass destruction as well as from the vagaries of nature.

SHELTERS IN PEACE TIME

Apart from terrorism, we are subject to varying emergencies based on acts of nature. In the United States, we experience emergencies as diverse as volcanic eruptions, hurricanes, windstorms, floods, lightning and ice storms, wild fires, and tornadoes. Each may require different preparations and different responses.

Thieves, looters and other societal predators can be as dangerous to our well being as terrorist weapons. People that live in high crime areas often put multiple locks on their doors as well as bars over their windows.

If you viewed the motion picture, "Panic Room," you are already familiar with the idea of a sophisticated secret room within a house that is designed to protect people from predators who might break in. Thousands of wealthy people have had such rooms built across America. The panic room depicted in the movie was extremely well designed and equipped. It would also have been incredibly costly. But, to provide the necessary thrills and chills to the viewer, it had built in flaws.

Fortunately, most of the preparations that you will make are not that costly. What's more, the preparations that you make for one kind of emergency will be useful in meeting many other kinds of emergencies.

OUR VERY SERIOUS CONCERN

Perhaps the greatest concern of every American should be that we have leaders of principle who will carry the fight to our enemies wherever they can be found. The second greatest concern is that every American take seriously the danger from weapons of mass destruction.

WMDs can take millions of lives while at the same time severely damaging our infrastructure and our economy. Your immediate concern should be how to protect your family and any others who look to you for guidance or protection. You need to take the initiative in setting aside any items that they might require during any emergency. What's more, you must strive to make available an appropriate shelter to protect them from diverse dangers.

Terrorists add a new ingredient to the mix, but their alchemy is similar enough to that of other natural threats that, in terms of home defense, we can almost knock off both birds with one stone. Or, to put it another way, one set of preparations provides for our need against many forms of natural disasters as well of many of the threats of terrorism.

The terrorist attacks on 9/11 took place during the morning rush hour when the terrorists knew that thousands of workers would be entering the World Trade Center. We can expect that most attacks of that nature will occur during business hours. In addition, it will be to the advantage of the terrorists to release a biological or a chemical agent when many people are on the streets or crowded into a target of opportunity. When terrorists crash jetliners into skyscrapers, they don't want those buildings to be vacant.

But, it doesn't much matter what time of day it is if they can successfully cause the meltdown of a nuclear reactor or detonate an atomic bomb. The resultant radioactive fallout will poison a huge area of the United States for a very long time.

SHOULD YOU CONSIDER A SHELTER?

Analyze your situation

You may live in an area where you face a real and continuing threat from natural disasters such as tornadoes, hurricanes, earthquakes, or terrorist attacks.

Yet you may assume that you live in a community where terrorism cannot touch you. But the possibility that they can detonate a nuclear device puts the entire continent at risk.

Does your community, your school district, fraternal organization, church, or employer provide a shelter at which you and your family are welcome, and which you can dependably reach within a few minutes?

Is that shelter safe and reliable from the threats for which it was prepared? Is it well stocked with fresh food, water, communications gear, first aid supplies, and other necessary items?

There are definite advantages to a community fallout shelter. First, it is likely that there will be people available who have diverse skills, from medical care to food preparation. On the other hand, the more people with whom you are involved, the less control you have over the way things are done, and the greater exposure to the spread of disease. So, while you will be in virtual control of what occurs within your own shelter, you are unlikely to hold much sway in a large public shelter.

Another important question is whether your family will be able to reach the public shelter before the emergency overtakes them or the shelter is closed.

Where Do You Spend Your Time

Of the 168 hours in each week, you may spend an hour a day in commuting to and from work and another nine hours at work. If you're a homemaker or working wife, you probably put more time in behind the wheel. Some people put in a lot more time at work, but for most of us it adds up to eleven hours a day, five days a week, or a total of fifty-five hours. That leaves another 113 hours remaining in the week. Most of those 113 hours are spent at home.

During the school year, the typical child spends about 128 hours at home. Teenagers probably spend only about 90 hours at home. Homemakers spend about 148 hours in the house, at the store, running kids to doctors as well as athletic and social functions. Those who have home businesses may spend 140 hours at home. In other words, most of us spend over half of our lives at home, including those seven or eight hours each night when we are abed and therefore not very conscious of events occurring around us.

Since you probably spend a great deal of your time at home, the likelihood of an attack occurring while you are there is proportionally higher. But even if an attack should occur while you are away from home, the logical place of rendezvous for your family is your home.

Since many of us own our homes, it is to our advantage us to make an investment in that home to protect ourselves from the effects of a WMD attack. For those who rent apartments, the preparation is just as important, though the investment must necessarily be limited.

You may feel overwhelmed by this discussion. Don't be. We'll take it a step at a time.

Do You Really Need a Shelter?

Why discuss the threat of nuclear weapons first? The answer is simple. If you can build a shelter to protect yourself to some degree from the dangers of a nuclear weapon, you will also have come a long way in protecting yourself from other serious dangers, including biological and chemical weapons, tornadoes and hurricanes, and, yes, human predators.

Remember, your family spends a great deal of time at home. If you prepare now, those members of your family who find themselves at home at the time of an attack—or who can reach home subsequent to an attack—will be able to move right into your shelter.

It's time to consider various methods of shielding yourself from these threats.

TYPES OF SHELTERS

Safe Rooms, Fallout Shelters and Blast Shelters

The type of shelter you will require depends upon the nature of the attack and your location in relationship to it. You might shelter in place in your office, your classroom, or on the lowest floor of your local mall. You might camp out in a tent, a trailer, or a motor home. You might actually sleep in your car. Or you might slide aside a bookcase to enter a specially prepared safe room in the center of your house or walk down a hidden tunnel to your underground blast shelter.

Safe Rooms

A safe room is a room within the house which may be reinforced to withstand the stress of tornado force winds, and even to exclude dangerous biotoxins or chemical gasses. It may also be designed to protect you from intruders. And it may be constructed to withstand severe blast and shock, and shielded to protect from the radiation produced by nuclear fallout.

Even a simple closet or bathroom can be quickly and inexpensively converted to a safe room. The retiring Director of the Department of Homeland Security, Tom Ridge, has shown concern that Americans have duct tape and a roll of polyethylene sheeting on hand to seal a room in order to protect themselves from biological and chemical agents.

Virtually all safe rooms, fallout shelters, and blast shelters can have filter systems economically installed that greatly reduce the risk of contamination by biotoxins.

Unless you live in the vicinity of a chemical plant or an oil refinery, you may be able to blissfully ignore the threat of chemical agents at home. But the danger exists for all who must move through heavily populated public facilities.

A system for detecting and excluding chemical contaminants is more complicated and far more expensive than a HEPA filter system designed to bar biological agents. It is unlikely, however, that terrorists will be able to produce enough chemical agents to effectively cover a broad geographic area. If they are not frustrated in their efforts to do so, they will probably release their chemical agents in densely populated areas and in facilities such as subway stations.

Blast and Fallout Shelters

A fallout shelter is not designed to withstand explosive force or intense heat. It is designed simply to keep out radiation.

A bomb or blast shelter is designed to resist the heat and explosive force of a bomb's detonation up to a few miles of ground zero.

If you live in a suburban or rural area, you are unlikely to experience the explosive shock, high winds, and enormous heat and radiation caused by a nuclear explosion. As a result, a basement or garage fallout shelter may be adequate.

But don't become complacent simply because you live in a rural area. If someone successfully detonates a nuclear weapon, or causes a nuclear power plant meltdown, there is high risk of radiation contamination to everyone in America. The risk is highest to those who live within a few hundred miles of the incident, because local winds will move the fallout to an fro.

But the risk is also extremely high for anyone living more or less east of the incident because the upper level winds will carry the fallout across the United States (and perhaps around the world), just as they did at Chernobyl.

The best shelters are sub-surface facilities constructed below the earth's surface and covered with three to six feet of earth. These shelters can be very expensive.

In the Event of a Nuclear Incident

(1) You must get into a shelter as soon as possible after any nuclear device is detonated. This shelter should have thick walls and a roof of concrete, preferably covered by several feet of earth. The door must be baffled with a similarly thick wall or door, so that radiation, traveling in a straight line, cannot enter the shelter. An absolute minimum of one foot of concrete is required, but if the radiation is powerful, one foot will not provide adequate protection. Many experts call for one foot of concrete covered by three to six feet of well-packed earth.

(2) Once you are in a shelter, you must determine the nature of the radioactive material by listening to radio broadcasts. Unfortunately, the authorities may never get that information to the emergency radio broadcasters. What's more, powerful radiation can destroy or interrupt radio transmissions. That's why, if possible your shelter should be equipped with a Geiger counter or a scintillation meter to check levels of radiation.

Caution: You must install an exterior radio antenna in order to receive broadcasts within a shelter. The heavy steel-reinforced concrete walls, covered with a foot or two of earth, may prevent the radio waves from reaching you.

(3) If a "dirty bomb" has been detonated in your area, sooner or later you are going to have to get out of that shelter and move away from the area of radiation because its power may continue unabated for many years.

(4) If it is not a dirty bomb, you should stay in shelter for two weeks, after which you should try to escape to an area free of contamination as directed by emergency authorities.

If you are out of doors when a nuclear device is triggered, you must try to get behind something dense and heavy, something like a concrete wall or a mound of earth. You must not look toward the detonation or you will be permanently blinded. It's best to be wrapped in white cloth or an aluminum space blanket, leaving no flesh uncovered, but when you have only a moment or two warning, such a luxury is unlikely.

After the explosion, there will be a great differential in air pressure, and an enormous shock wave will roll out for miles from ground zero. You must remain under cover until after this shock wave and wind passes. It can roll cars over and knock down buildings. As soon as possible, you must get indoors, into a makeshift shelter as described below. But, before you do, you must hose or shower the radioactive dust off yourself, particularly your hair, nose, ears and mouth, and you must discard all of your clothing. This is vital to your survival.

Blast Shelters

A bomb shelter is designed to resist the heat and explosive force of a bomb's detonation. Depending upon the type and size of weapon, the occupants might survive within as little as a few yards, or be vaporized as far away as a miles from ground zero. In the case of a car bomb, for example, a sub-surface shelter would offer significant protection to occupants twenty yards away. In the event of a 5-Megaton Hydrogen Bomb, the thought of being a full ten miles away would still be terrifying.

Fallout Shelters

A fallout shelter is not designed to stand up under explosive force or intense heat. Its purpose is simply to keep out radiation, but because of the mass required to keep out radiation, a fallout shelter is also generally quite sturdy.

A shelter built of loosely laid up solid concrete blocks within a garage may provide protection against radiation, but not against blast, shock waves, or biological and chemical agents because the seams between the blocks would permit them to enter.

CONSIDER BUILDING

Consider some of these shelter types:

- 1. An Interior Room Conversion, basement or garage fallout shelter, for protection from biological and chemical agents, and nuclear radiation
- 2. Attached above ground fallout shelter, for protection against nuclear radiation and biological and chemical agents
- 3. A sub-surface bomb and fallout shelter, for protection against blast, nuclear radiation, and biological and chemical agents.

INTERIOR SAFE ROOMS

If you're building a new house, you may build an interior shelter of reinforced concrete that would be suitable for nuclear, biological and chemical weapon protection. You may also retrofit an existing interior room, such as a walk-in closet, to make it safe from biological and chemical agents.

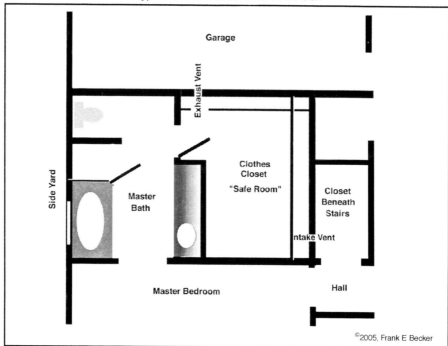

Typical Closet to Safe Room Conversion

©2005, Frank E Becker

A shelter built of loosely laid up solid concrete blocks can be constructed within a garage that may provide protection against all WMDs, but not against blast and shock waves. A new wrinkle on the Civil Defense design of the 1960s is to coat both the outside and inside walls with fiberglass cloth and an epoxy resin that bonds the blocks and is actually stronger than blocks laid up with mortar. To bring the shelter up to date, add a HEPA filter to filter out biological contaminants. Add a shut off valve or cap for the air intake to keep out chemical gasses. Add an oxygen supply to protect inhabitants over a short period if the room must be tightly sealed against chemical agents.

See Appendix B for instructions on installing a HEPA intake filter and exhaust system in a first floor or basement room in your home.

Safe Room Filter Vent System

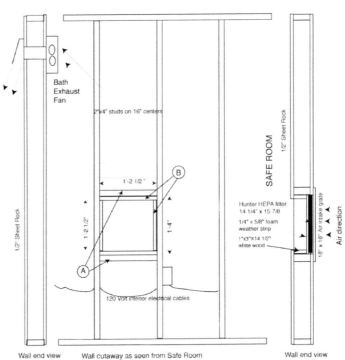

When a safe room is constructed as part of a new house, it is relatively inexpensive to pour reinforced concrete footings, floor, walls and roof, thus making it nearly impregnable and resistant to radiation. Add a well-designed external HVAC system, and a HEPA filter, and your family has instant day or night access to a reliable safe room.

Check the FEMA's website (www.fema.gov) for instructions on constructing a safe room from scratch, or for converting and hardening an existing room to protect against nuclear, biological and chemical weapons, as well as unwanted intruders.

FALLOUT SHELTERS

Fallout shelters have sufficient mass to protect you from a measurable amount of radiation. As a rule, they will not satisfactorily protect from blast and heat.

Again, check FEMA's website for designs and specifications for safe rooms, tornado and hurricane shelters, fallout shelters and blast shelters.

Garage Fallout Shelter

Check FEMA (www.fema.gov) for garage shelter designs and standards. There are many other websites offering hundreds of plans. Check with your building contractor or an engineer before proceeding. The roofs of many poorly constructed shelters from the 1960s have since collapsed.

Basement Fallout Shelter

The basement shelter has been denigrated because it poses the threat of asphyxiation to its occupants if the house should catch on fire or if there should be a natural gas or other chemical leak nearby. Basements are also generally damp and chilly and will promote pneumonia and other lung diseases. To their credit, they are generally easily accessible, easily protected from others, protected by earth on all sides, and can be inexpensively constructed.

A basement shelter that is well insulated by numerous layers of masonry can be made air tight. Exterior intake and exhaust vents can be installed that may provide an excellent shelter.

What's more, the likelihood of the house catching on fire is small, unless set by vandals.

BLAST SHELTERS

While a fallout shelter will not help protect you from a bomb's explosive force, a blast shelter will. And, because of its mass, a blast shelter will also protect from radiation.

Attached Fallout Shelter

An attached shelter can be built above ground and adjacent to your house of reinforced concrete, then earth-bermed. It will also serve as a shelter from other WMDs. Because it is not within the structure of the house, it is not subject to burning or becoming an "oven" because the house cannot burn down around it.

Floor plan: Add-on or Attached Shelter

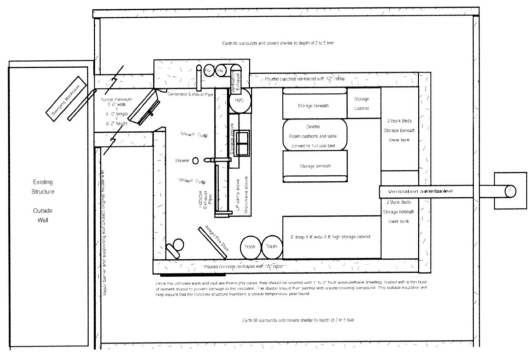

Free Standing Fallout Shelter

A free standing shelter is similar to an attached shelter, but requires you to leave the house to enter it. Again, FEMA has a very nice design for a free-standing shelter. The problem is, the walls need to be much thicker or earth-bermed in order to keep out radiation.

Fall Out Shelter Entrances

All fallout shelters must have some sort of a baffling system to keep radiation from entering the shelter. You may construct massive walls, but if you only install a 2-inch thick metal fire door, radiation will penetrate it and harm all occupants. Unless the door is as thick as the walls, which is impractical, the door must have a wall in front of it to keep the deadly rays out.

The diagram opposite illustrates how this can be done. It is very costly. Whether you decide on a wall that is 12 inches, 24 inches, or 36 inches thick, the walls and the roof must be of a uniform thickness. The interior is only as secure as the thinnest shielding wall.

Blast Shelter Baffle System and Rolling Blast Door

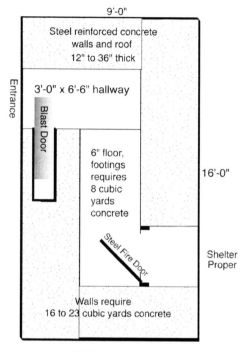

WMD Shelter Lock

Frank Becker
10/07/2002

The Sub-Surface Fallout Shelter

If one is concerned about radiation, one might consider a below ground shelter, similar to the one I designed for our family during the Cuban Missile Crisis. That shelter was twenty-feet in diameter, with a small room for a toilet and shower, and a long, angled tunnel leading to our basement. It is situated in New York's Mid-Hudson Valley. It had it's own water well and water pump, with a 200 gallon water storage tank, septic system, electrical generator (including a buried 275-gallon gasoline tank), massive, fallout proof air vents, and a cunningly designed massive steel reinforced vault-type door to keep intruders out. A picture of the shelter and entrance tunnel is displayed on page 141.

Cutaway of a Proposed Sub-Surface Blast and Fallout Shelter

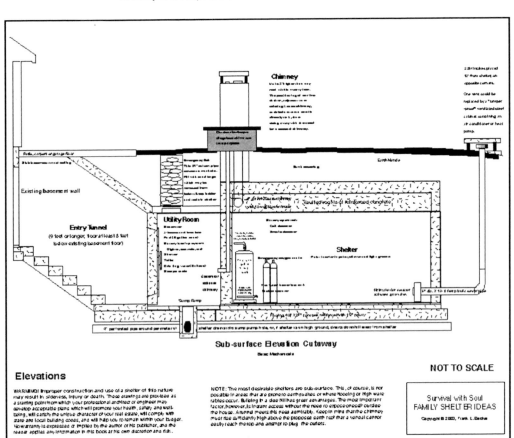

Most people spend twelve hours out of every twenty-four in or near their homes, so they are properly the first choice for sheltering if terror or tornado strikes.

The sub-surface blast shelter provides significant protection again blast and heat, as well as protection from nuclear radiation. Additional equipment can be added to the access doors and the air vents to protect against biological and chemical agents.

15. Shelter Engineering Issues

Engineering Issues

Many thousands of safe rooms and shelters have been constructed by concerned Americans. For obvious reasons, the people who make such preparations prefer not to make their preparations public.

If you are interested, check the web for ideas and builders who specialize in these structures. If possible, deal with established local builders. Better construction companies will be able to assist in planning and building your safe room. Consider having a professional architect or engineer create drawings for your builder.

The drawing on the preceding page will give you an idea of the complexity of a sub-surface shelter. It's not simply a place to survive, but a hardened shell that keeps out unpleasant things while providing you with the basics of life which are generally taken for granted. These include air, light, water, heating and cooling, and waste removal. This drawing is not provided as a design for your shelter.

WARNING! Improper construction and use of a sub-surface shelter may result in sickness, injury or death. These drawings are provided to demonstrate the complexity and sample layout of a shelter. Consult your professional architect or engineer for acceptable plans that will promote your health, safety and well-being, will satisfy the unique character of your real estate, will comply with state and local building codes, and will help you to remain within your budget. No warranty is expressed or implied by the author or his publisher, and the reader applies any information in this book at his own discretion and risk.While you should make certain that all your work meets or exceeds state and local building codes, there is some debate over whether a building permit is required or whether a shelter is taxable as real estate.

The conclusions drawn forty years ago were that shelters may be kept secret for the best interests of their owners, and that, in most municipalities, permits were not sought nor required.

You are advised to consult an attorney or speak with your local code official. As a rule, tax collectors hate to let an "opportunity" for added revenue pass them by. You will require a very large yard in order to build a sub-surface shelter. When digging down eight or ten feet, the hole required will be very large, and the piles of excavated dirt will spill outward from the hole.

You might want to consider an above ground shelter. FEMA has some great designs. Keep in mind that their walls and roof are very thin, so you might want to have a shelter redesigned with thicker walls and roof, and perhaps even earth bermed.

Warning: Before you dig, check with your utility company to prevent cutting cables or pipelines.

SUB-SURFACE SHELTER FEATURES

A sub-surface shelter is obviously not suitable for coastal areas, places subject to flooding, or areas where ground water is near the surface. The main features of a shelter are discussed below in alphabetical order.

Bomb Shelter Access Tunnel Under Construction, 1962

The author's brother, John Becker, a brilliant engineer and artisan, is shown standing in the 30 foot access tunnel leading from the basement of the family house to the 400 square foot sub-surface shelter. Directly behind John is the alcove designed to house the electrical generator and LP gas tanks. The curving tunnel to the right is an air exhaust channel to the chimney of the house. Natural convection currents continually change the air in the forty year old structure. The steel reinforced concrete vault door, with its four bolts inserted into the frame is in the upper left. The picture was taken from atop the shelter's 12" thick reinforced concrete roof. This roof was later covered with two feet of earth and sod.

Access Tunnels

The tunnel should have a reinforced steel fire door where it enters the basement of the house. This door should have double dead bolts to keep intruders from entering the tunnel. Should they, however, get into the tunnel, there might be a second, bank vault type door between the tunnel and the shelter. This door is designed as much to keep out radioactivity as it is to keep out intruders.

Make certain that the tunnel turns at a sharp angle en route from basement to shelter. If radioactive materials should enter the basement of the house, their rays may enter the tunnel, but will be absorbed by the tunnel wall where it turns. No one should be allowed to enter this part of the tunnel if there is a possibility that there is radioactive material in the basement of the house.

Tunnel with offset or baffle to stop radiation

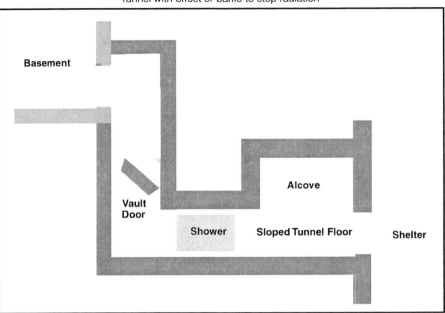

A patio or carport slab adjacent to the house can act as the ceiling of the access tunnel partway to the shelter. You may excavate to the edge of the carport with a backhoe or front-end loader. Dig out the remainder of the tunnel with a Bobcat or similar front end loader, but expect to do a lot of pick and shovel work.

Warning. Do not park vehicles on above the tunnel or shelter roof unless they are engineered and reinforced to bear the weight.

Rent a power saw with a masonry blade to cut a door opening through the concrete wall between the tunnel and the basement. You might want to have a locking metal fire door installed here. Use foam weather stripping to make doors airtight. The basement door should open into the tunnel. On the basement side of the opening, you might want to build wooden shelves that can be hinged so that they disguise the opening.

It will probably be necessary to have a ramp or staircase down from the basement of the house to the shelter in order to situate the shelter at an adequate depth. The tunnel walls may be of block or poured concrete. The Footings, floor and roof are of reinforced concrete.

All entry areas must have baffle walls, or zig zags, to prevent radiation and blast shock waves from penetrating straight into the shelter.

Cooking and water heating

You are familiar with LP gas tanks that are attached to backyard barbecue units. LP gas is a heavier-than-air, highly explosive petroleum product. There is a risk to using it in a closed shelter beneath the earth. It has the advantage that it is stored on your premises while, if there is an interruption in electricity, you may have no source of energy.

If your shelter is well ventilated, and the gas system is carefully designed and installed, it can provide a convenient means to heat the shelter, cook food and heat wash water. The LP tank should be located away from the shelter in case of fire or explosion. it should be installed by a professional using the newer reinforced plastic lines. Black iron pipe will rust. Copper tubing will corrode if it comes in contact with concrete. You may want to build a separate, well-ventilated, concrete block cabinet for a 100-pound tank.

Check out your local RV dealer to see how the industry has refined these lovely little vehicles over the past fifty years so that occupants may cook, heat water, refrigerate, and warm the RV with gas.

You might prefer to use the small gas burners and fuel tanks carried by back packers and campers. Take caution, however, because even a one pound cylinder has enormous explosive force.

Decor

Paint the interior of the tunnel and shelter in pale yellows and light greens because they are pleasant, relaxing, and most ideal for people under stress. If you have any extra pictures of landscapes and pleasant scenes, hang them in the shelter. You might also hang a dart board for diversion, and make games and books available. Always store items in moisture proof bags.

Detectors

Make certain that you have smoke detectors and carbon monoxide detectors in the basement of your house, as well as in the entry tunnel and in your shelter proper. You will need to detect the source of any problem as soon as possible so that you can deal with it, either by sealing a leak or shutting the airtight doors between the basement and your shelter.

The wealthier and more creative among us may be able to secure detectors for the outside of the shelter that will shut the vents if tiny quantities of deadly chemicals or biological agents are detected.

Drainage

Have your builders install 4" perforated pipe around the perimeter at the base of the shelter and drain it by gravity into a remote sump hole. If the shelter is on a hill side or high ground, it can be made to drain downhill away from the shelter. Don't rely on public sewers to pump away your waste. Their pumps may fail and sewers lines may back up into your shelter.

Electrical supply

If you own a reliable electrical generator, specifically a well ventilated, 100% duty-cycle machine, and can provide an adequate piped-in fuel supply, you may operate a lighting system, refrigerator, ventilator fans, and even a sump pump to protect the shelter from unexpected water problems.

You cannot rule out anything. Murphy's Law states that if anything can go wrong, it will. It's best to keep things simple.

A generator may be installed in an alcove in the entry tunnel, but it should be exhausted to the outdoors through heavy iron pipe. Make certain that the exhaust cannot easily be reached or jammed with rags by vandals.

You may also opt to install a separate electrical entry system from the street or house into your shelter. You can have a cutaway installed that will shut off the connection from the power company's supply line and immediately kick in your generator to maintain the flow of electricity.

You might install a system of storage batteries in the hallway outside the shelter proper, so that any fumes will not penetrate the shelter and create problems. These batteries can be on continual trickle charge, and can have a converter attached which will allow you to have 120-volt lights inside both the shelter and tunnel for an extended period, even if the generator fails.

Lead acid batteries, such as used in automobiles, also present a danger. If salt water, or various other chemicals, reaches the acid, they will generate deadly gases, such as chlorine.

Emergency Air Supply

You may be able to get a tank of compressed air from a local industrial gas distributor, but be aware that the air will not be pure and is not recommended for breathing. On the other hand, if you have to shut your shelter off from outside air, a tank of highly compressed air or oxygen could be a lifesaver.

Warning, there must be absolutely no spark or flame where oxygen is being used. Early in the space program, NASA used pure oxygen in a space capsule, and three of our bravest and best were incinerated along with everything else in the capsule that would burn. A stream of oxygen, mixed with acetylene or other combustible gas, will easily cut a one inch thick piece of steel in two.

Emergency Exit

There must be an alternative emergency exit that is difficult for predators to locate, yet enables you to exit the shelter even if you are weak from illness. This exit must also be baffled so that it bars the entry of radiation or contaminated air. You must have the necessary tools on hand to break out of the structure if necessary. In this case, a short length of 30" culvert pipe can run out the wall of the shelter, then another piece can be set vertically to serve as manhole.

As an alternative, you can build the 36" vertical pipe inside the shelter, running it right through the roof to the surface. This exit shaft should be filled with sand bags to block radiation. Plan to drag the bags out into the shelter if it becomes necessary to use that exit because the main tunnel becomes blocked.

Keep a ladder and tools in the shelter to aid in an emergency escape. You might build an outdoor barbecue to disguise the true purpose of the shelter's chimneys.

Furniture

Your choice of furniture will depend on your attitude toward the shelter. If it is dry and clean, you can make a very pleasant getaway where you can go to read or simply be alone. A clean, dry, properly ventilated shelter might be used as a family recreation room.

Certainly, regardless of the furniture, you want to conduct periodic drills where the entire family spends a night, or even a weekend in the shelter. It can be treated like any special activity, whether a camp out or a day trip. You can even have pajama parties for the kids. These drills are the ideal way to expose any weaknesses in your preparations or flaws in your shelter design.

If the room is strictly utilitarian, knock together some bunks out of 2x4s and plywood. Keep sleeping bags rolled up and sealed in airtight bags. Pillows are a nice addition if you can keep them dry and clean.

A folding table and chairs makes a good set up for eating and playing games, yet can be put away for periods of calisthenics and other exercise.

You can pick up some old cabinets for storage and to set up your kitchen. Use a portable camp stove for cooking, and a plastic wash basin for dishes. Try to use paper products wherever possible. Keep a store of plastic bags on hand for the trash, and, when safe, carry it to the end of the tunnel. Beware fire hazards and rodents. A stack of metal trash cans with tight fitting lids will be handy for temporary disposal.

If you want to be more elaborate, check out the way RV manufacturers squeeze every inch out of their vehicles, and how stylish and even luxurious they make them. Take a page out of their book when you design built-ins. If you have sufficient electric current, you can use a microwave or toaster oven to prepare meals.

If you plan to house a lot of people, try breaking up the area so that you have both a men's and women's dorm area, but don't interrupt the flow of air from inlet to exhaust. By setting up two or three sets of bunk beds in each area, you can sleep a lot more people. If the ceiling is high enough, you can stack three people in a bunk. Put those that prefer cooler sleeping at he bottom.

Heat, ventilation, and air-conditioning (HVAC)

Ideally, you will install a heat pump or air conditioner in any shelter, and operate it using house current. This will keep the shelter at the desirable temperature and humidity. If there is an emergency, the shelter mass will be heated to the appropriate temperature and will not cool or heat rapidly.

The air conditioner will remove dampness. Thick concrete walls may take years to cure and will be emitting vapor over that period. In addition, a sub-surface shelter tends to be damp because of ground water. If you do not have water problems, you can keep the shelter dry by running an air conditioner in moist weather, then running an electric heater during the winter.

If you are not able to afford an air conditioning system, consider installing a dehumidifier that drains outside the shelter.

If you install HEPA filters in a properly designed duct system, you can bring in air without bringing in fallout or biological elements. If, however, chemical toxins are released nearby, you will have to have a way of detecting them and shutting the shelter vents off from the outside world.

Sub-surface shelter air intake vent

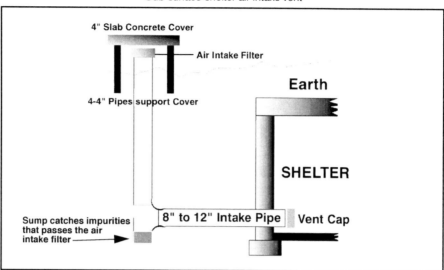

You might want to make it a policy to shut all air vents for the first hour after an attack, or until you receive information that it is safe to reopen them. If, for example, a terrorist releases a relatively small amount of toxic material in a congested area, he can harm many people. In the countryside, however, toxins would be quickly dissipated.

Roof

The roofs on sub-surface shelters and tunnels should be at least one-foot thick and of steel-reinforced concrete. At least two additional feet of packed earth should be spread above. In order to be truly effective against radiation, the more earth, the better. There is little point in spending the amount of money required for a shelter of this nature unless you intend to make it effective against radiation and against intrusion.

Roofs should be vaulted or hemispheric in shape, poured concrete over rebar, with supporting posts designed to withstand shock and weight. This is a determination best left to professional engineers, though you may get significant help from various websites and may even find engineers who will share their evaluations at no charge. Remember, an engineers skill is his stock in trade, and a worker is worthy of his hire.

Warning. Wet concrete can weight several thousand pounds per cubic yard. Pouring the roof of a shelter can be very dangerous work. If it collapses, people can be killed. Even if no one is harmed, you will still find yourself with a foot or two of expensive concrete covering the floor of your unfinished shelter. Make certain that this work is done by experienced professionals. John Becker placed over one hundred 2x4 studs vertically to support the plywood forms on our 20 foot diameter shelter. He also placed a lally column in the center of the structure with reinforcing rods radiating out to the perimeter, as well as a layer of 6" steel mesh.

Before covering the roof with earth, you may wish to place a layer of urethane foam sheets atop it as an insulator. You might also want to brush on a coat of roofing tar and put down a layer of rolled roofing to keep out ground water. Consult your local building supplier for advice on installing a "built up roof."

Sewer System

You must take special care to get rid of human waste.

You can use a metal pail with a tight fitting cover, as a toilet. Line the pail with a heavy plastic bag, and, after use, seal it the bag tightly and lower it carefully into a garbage can that has a tight fitting lid. Store this can up the tunnel away from the shelter proper.

As an alternative, you might buy a portable toilet, but you will still face the question of where to empty it.

You can install a toilet and build your own septic tank. You might be able to hook up to the existing septic system if you install a special sump pump that will move the effluent uphill to that tank. But if power fails, the pump won't work.

If you want to build your own septic system adjacent to your in-ground shelter, you will require a large back yard. You can make numerous punctures with a cold chisel in a used 275-gallon oil tank, then bury it in a bed of crushed stone outside the shelter and below the level of the shelter floor, for use as short term emergency septic tank. Simply run a 4" plastic waste line out under the floor and insert it into the tank. Drop this pipe 1/4" per foot of length. Consult an engineer or septic tank installer.

Then you can safely install a conventional house toilet. It would be nice to hook a water supply up to the toilet, but remember that you will only be able to flush the toilet about a hundred times before the tank is full. Four people in a shelter will easily flush the toilet a total of twelve times a day, so the tank would be full in less than a week.

To conserve water, you could simply pour a bucket of water into the toilet to flush it. Don't use a makeshift septic system for regular use. It must be reserved for a true emergency.

Practice good hygiene and make certain that everyone cleans their hands and fingernails after using the toilet.

Shower

Install a shower head in the wall or ceiling of the tunnel. Put it close to the shelter, beyond the turn in the tunnel, so that users will not be exposed to potential radiation from the basement. Install a shower pan in the tunnel floor so that the drain water won't run down the slope into the shelter. Drain it into your septic system. Hang a shower curtain to keep the water in the shower pan.

When people enter the shelter, have them leave their clothes in the upper tunnel, or even in the basement, and make them shower off very quickly but thoroughly, especially their hair, ears, etc.

Keep fresh towels, underwear and warm clothing sealed in well-labeled, air tight plastic bags on shelves by the shower. When they enter the shelter, they will be clean, dry, and hopefully free of dangerous contaminants.

Water Heaters

Consider an electric water heater. You could add a second water heater for your house and shelter, installing it in the alcove in the entry tunnel. Run the cold water supply line from the house. Then install a tee at the top of the water heater, with shut off valves, that will allow you to direct the hot water back up the tunnel through insulated pipes to the main water heater in the house. That way, you will have two water heaters sharing the demands of the family. In the event of an emergency, you would shut off the hot water line to the house so that the hot water in the new tank would be available only for use in the shelter.

Even if the energy source is interrupted, you can mix the 30 gallons of hot water with cold in order to shower everyone entering the shelter.

Warning! If you are considering installing gas appliances, remember that they will be drawing large quantities of oxygen from the shelter, oxygen that you might not be able to reliably replace because you have to limit the inflow of air. Gas is also highly explosive and, in a closed atmosphere, may asphyxiate the occupants.

16. Impromptu Shelters

The most daunting challenge to anyone caught in the vicinity of a natural disaster or a terrorist attack is deciding when and where to shelter.

The potential variety and scope of these events is impossible to forecast. For that reason, some of the shelters described below may sound like some of those over-the-top solutions to worst case scenarios. But when your life is at stake, and no advance preparation has been possible, you will need to be alert to workable alternatives.

IMPROVISE

If any portion of this book will cause it to be labeled fear mongering, this is probably it. Sherman is quoted, "War is hell!" May God grant that the horror of WMDs does not touch our shores.

Depending upon the kind of emergency, you might shelter in your home, auto, tent, RV, basement, a public rest room, cave, cellar, culvert pipe, ditch, boat, highway underpass, subway station, tunnel, storm sewer, or whatever else may be available or appropriate.

As a rule, the deeper below ground you can get, the safer you are from a variety of dangers, including blast, radiation, and tornadoes.

On the other hand, both flood waters and deadly heavier-than-air gasses will collect in depressions and seep downward. So, you will not be safe from chemical toxins unless your chosen shelter is carefully sealed and properly ventilated. Nor is it safe to go below ground to escape an earthquake.

NUCLEAR THREATS AND RADIOACTIVITY

Imagine, if you will, that you learn of a nuclear incident 30 miles upwind of you. Perhaps it's the result of a meltdown at a nuclear power plant or the detonation of a conventional nuclear weapon. You will need to decide whether to get under cover as soon as possible or to try to leave the area. If you decide to shelter in place, you must be prepared to remain there for at least one, and probably two weeks. Run or hide. Those are your only alternatives for survival.

Once you make that decision—either to hunker down or to run—you must give each member of your family or group, especially children, a potassium iodine tablet to reduce the risk of absorbing deadly radioactive elements into their thyroids.

If you are equipped with an Auto Pack, you can point your car somewhere and "Go!" But you must act quickly because prevailing winds could sweep a radioactive cloud many miles in a matter of seconds, and sweep them into the atmosphere in a matter of minutes, so that they are spread over an enormous area in a matter of days. And if you are driving a car, you must expect to meet other drivers who are unprepared mentally, physically or spiritually for this emergency. They will panic and cause accidents that result in highway congestion and ultimate gridlock. Stay off the heavily traveled highways and the Interstate system. Look for alternate passable routes.

Every major war has had its refugees wandering aimlessly from place to place, clogging the highways, vying for food, shelter, and medical care. This book encourages you to prepare for emergencies so that you do not become a victim and may even come to the assistance of one less fortunate.

If you have a well-stocked shelter, constructed of sufficient mass to shield you from fallout, you should shelter in place and not attempt the highways.

Conventional Nuclear Weapon

The closer to the ground a nuclear weapon is detonated, the more earth will be scooped up by the explosion and turned into a cloud of radioactive fallout. Such a cloud may be carried over your area with the heavier particles falling out and collecting on the ground nearer ground zero. Further out from the detonation, the fallout will be lighter and relatively less dangerous. Relatively less dangerous, but still dangerous! Depending upon the radioactive elements of which the bomb was composed, the radioactivity may decay rapidly enough that you dare leave your shelter within two weeks.

Don't be fooled. You can not see, taste, or smell radioactivity. It causes a horrible death, and, among those who survive, it may result in cancer and other terrible diseases.

If you do not have a fallout shelter, and a conventional nuclear weapon or atom bomb is detonated within fifty miles, you should try to escape the area. In the event of a nuclear power plant meltdown, you should probably try to escape toward the area downwind of the power plant. If a "dirty bomb" has been detonated, you must immediately escape the area.

The direction you travel will depend upon the kind of radioactive threat with which you are dealing. The local winds may be in any direction. Move away from them. Once the radioactive materials have reached the upper atmosphere, the prevailing winds will generally carry them from west to the east. If possible, you will move northeast or southeast away from their path. Listen to your car radio for emergency instructions.

Nuclear Power Plant Meltdown

The characteristics of a nuclear power plant meltdown are significantly different from the detonation of a nuclear weapon. As with the Chernobyl catastrophe, a power plant may continue to spew toxic clouds over your area for months or years. Hunkering down in your shelter will just put off the inevitable escape through an increasingly dangerous radioactive field.

It's not a matter of the luck of the toss. It's a matter of understanding the dangers that you face and exercising the wisdom God gives you.

Dirty Bombs

Dirty bombs may be triggered by just a few sticks of dynamite. So if your area should be struck by a rash of car bombings, the detonation of a dirty bomb may not even get the immediate attention of the authorities. They won't realize they have a problem until the needle on a Geiger Counter hits the pin.

The terrorist's goal is to use a small explosive charge to disperse a deadly radioactive substance that they may have stolen from a local hospital or laboratory. The explosion would produce a cloud of radioactive debris that might cover only a few city blocks, but is so toxic that life will not be possible in that area for thousands of years. You must not shelter near the detonation of a dirty bomb. You must escape as quickly as you can, wearing whatever protective gear you can devise.

An exception presents itself if government rescue workers can reach you—and perhaps thousands of others—and outfit you with protective clothing before you inhale, ingest or are heavily exposed to the contamination. Some would consider this possibility as highly unlikely.

THE GREAT ESCAPE

Your automobile offers little protection from radiation or deadly gasses. It will, however, help keep you safe from radioactive particles that would otherwise settle directly onto your body or be inhaled into your lungs. If you have an SUV, or a car like mine in which the back seat folds down to offer access to the trunk, you can get to your survival items without even opening the driver's door.

This is important whether you are evacuating and are warned not to exit your car, or you use your car to try to stay safe from biotoxins in the atmosphere.

You might drive your car into a quarry, park it next to a sand bank, and then try to cover most, of the car without being buried alive. If you are able to improvise a safe way to enter and leave the car, it might be a serviceable fallout shelter.

Biotoxins and Chemical Agents

If you shut off your car ventilation system and park in the shade, you may be safe if you remain inside until the toxin ends its life span. In addition, dangerous chemical agents may be dissipated by the wind.

If you have them available, fit gas masks, or at least surgical face masks, to each passenger. Do not count on the security of your car. Head as far away from the source as the problem as rapidly as you possible can, keeping the vehicle tightly sealed.

Once you have left the danger area, try to flush one another off with a hose to get rid of any particles or toxins. Do not remove protective gear until you have thoroughly flushed one another off, then remove all clothing and continue the process. A few drops of household bleach in a gallon of water, poured over the head of each person, will help destroy any biological toxins.

Remember, it's okay to shelter in place with a lot of people in the event of a nuclear threat, but you may want to isolate your family if there is an attack with biotoxins. Only one infected person can spread a disease very quickly.

IMPROMPTU SHELTERS

Once you have made the decision to evacuate, and have left the danger area, you must begin looking for a place to shelter. If you have not made arrangements with friends or relatives outside your area to stay with them, or if they too had to evacuate because of the emergency, you will have to find a place to stay until authorities allow you to return home. Make no mistake about it. During a terrorist emergency, authorities will have the power to dictate where and when you travel.

Here are some possible places of shelter with descriptions of how they might be exploited.

Auto

The principal purpose for your automobile or truck is to escape from the area of imminent danger. Your vehicle is your first means of escape from the disaster area. Unfortunately, in the event of a biological attack, your government may refuse to allow you to evacuate the area.

Then your actions are a matter of judgment. You might feel safest around those whom you assume have not been contaminated. If possible, head for home and the safe room that hopefully you will have created. Remember, you can make a safe room in your house using a sheet of polyethylene and a roll of duct tape if nothing more sophisticated is at hand.

See Appendix B for a suggested ventilation system that you can install in a walk-in closet or bedroom for about one hundred dollars.

A basement or cellar is a safer place to hide from blast and fallout than is a ground level room. But it will not protect you from fire, fumes or flood.

The basement of a large masonry building, especially a multi-story building, has the advantage of a number of layers of concrete above your head, helping to keep out radiation. Think in terms of sheltering in utility areas and bathrooms which may have water supplies but do not generally have windows. They are often near the safer center of the structure.

Boat or Ship

If you own a fair sized boat, you can put to sea to escape biotoxins as well as chemical agents. In the even of a nuclear incident, the radioactive dust falling on the decks may be flushed off using seawater from a hose or a bucket. The radiation that emanates from particles that sink to the bottom of the sea will not reach the hull of your vessel.

Cave

While a cave is generally ideal for escaping nuclear radiation, it is also often a damp, dark, cold, and depressing place where one is subject to rapid loss of body heat and the danger of pneumonia. An inadequate supply of fresh air and water may also prove a problem.

The location of most caves is known to a lot of people, particularly spelunkers or cave explorers, and so they are apt to rapidly fill with people who have the same idea as you. Consider a cave to escape nuclear radiation.

Culvert pipe

Main highways have large culvert pipes passing beneath them wherever a water must cross under. On the interstate system, these pipes are often more than fifty feet long and six and eight feet high. During a dry spell, the center of one of these pipes is an excellent place to find temporary shelter from radiation. In the even of a cloud burst, however, one could easily be swept away and drowned. You need to be concerned about flash floods, excessive cold, insects, snakes and marauding animals.

Ditches

Watch any war movie, from any era, and you will probably see people diving into ditches and trenches to avoid exploding bombs and strafing aircraft. A ditch remains a good place to go if you have limited foreknowledge of an impending bomb blast. But an open ditch will not protect you from radioactive fallout or other WMDs.

Highway Underpasses

During the Cold War, New York's Governor Nelson Rockefeller was derided because he wanted to construct bomb shelters beneath the overpasses on the New York State Thruway.

While such shelters were never developed, highway underpasses may still offer limited protection from blast and radioactive fallout.

If, in the event of an imminent nuclear detonation, you find yourself near a major highway interchange, drive your car up the slope beneath the center of the overpass bridge until your hood and roof almost touch the bridgework. It will offer some protection from the blast and should limit the amount of radioactive dust that settles on your roof. What's more, you will have more than a foot of concrete and steel above your head to help stop the radiation. You may be able to survive simply by remaining locked in your car beneath the concrete and steel above your head. Remember, most bridges have enormous beams supporting the roadway, so when you pull up between those beams, they too are acting as barriers to the radioactivity.

Driving your car under the structure of an overpass will certainly be considered an illegal activity in times of peace. In time of war, however, if you're not injuring anyone else, or blocking the highway, you may want to look out for your family's survival first, then worry about a parking ticket.

Highway Tunnels

It will probably be frowned upon if you cause a traffic jam by stopping your car in the Holland Tunnel. In fact, in the midst of an emergency, count on the tunnel being closed to traffic. It remains, however, that tunnels are excellent places to escape the radiation from a nuclear weapon. Unfortunately, many automobile tunnels are so contaminated with carbon monoxide that they are not viable choices for sheltering.

Public Rest Rooms

This will definitely not be a favorite place to hunker down, but many rest rooms in public malls and office buildings are located on the lower floors and toward the inside of the structures. These rest rooms are often enveloped with walls and roofs of masonry, thus protecting from radioactivity.

If you have household disinfectant with you, or you can access the building's janitorial supplies, you can swab down the walls, floors and fixtures, rinse them thoroughly, and have a fairly safe place to reside.

Recreational Vehicle

Those who saw the movie, "Independence Day," will remember the scene of hundreds of RVs parked in the middle of a salt flat. An RV is self-contained. Although it isn't recommended that you try to tow or drive one in the heavy traffic generated by panic during a terrorist attack, you might leave one parked in a remote area so that it can be your home away from home. (Of course, you may find that someone has taken your home-away-from-home away from you when you finally arrive there.)

Storm or Root Cellar

The midwestern storm cellar is the time tested place for escaping tornadoes and violent storms. Many people furnish them with beds and other comforts so that they can spend entire days or nights beneath the ground, avoiding the deadly storms.

If these shelters are properly ventilated, and a baffled entry system is added to stop radiation, they make excellent blast and fallout shelters.

Storm Sewer

A storm sewer is a relatively clean underground system of large pipes, generally accessed from man holes, that might provide a short-term shelter from nuclear radiation. Expect to be visited by creatures like scorpions, snakes and spiders, and avoid going underground if there is an impending storm.

Subway Station

As the Japanese will testify, a subway station is not a good place to hide during a chemical attack with Ricin, but it is an excellent place to hide from nuclear radiation.

During the Blitz, hundreds of thousands of London's citizens escaped to the "Underground" each night to avoid Hitler's bombs.

Tent

Okay, a tent won't protect you from much of anything except rain, wind and cold. But that's the entire point. If you have escaped the area of danger, a tent will help protect you from the elements and may save your life. Include one in your Auto Pack.

CONCLUSION

No one can provide you with an exhaustive list of scenarios nor provide a ready made solution for each one. If you find yourself questioning these ideas, or coming up with solutions of your own, it indicates that you have begun to coolly appraise potential dangers, and to arrive at solutions. Congratulations! You have taken the first step in finding your own impromptu shelters.

STEP 7,

Prepare Yourself and Your Loved Ones

17. Prepare Yourself

Many people believe that it's impossible to prepare for something like a terrorist attack. But it isn't hopeless and the preparations aren't overwhelming.

In fact, when you take it one step at a time, it's not difficult at all. What's more, it can and must be accomplished. Your life, the lives of your loved ones, and in a sense the well being of our entire nation is at stake.

Your preparations have a broad purpose. For while you are preparing for terrorism, you're simultaneously preparing for a multitude of other potential disasters as well.

Most of the suggestions offered in this book will help you through this important process of preparing yourself for a multitude of emergencies.

YOUR BODY

It's important that you take care of your body, regardless of whether you believe that we face natural emergencies or terrorist attacks. If you are not healthy and do not exercise regularly, you will not look or feel as good as you should, and you will be less able to seize the opportunities that come your way.

Watch What You Eat and Drink

First, take the advice of nutritionists, doctors and personal trainers. Get in shape! Get some of the fat and sugar out of your system. Don't succumb to those crash diets that must inevitably follow one after another. But if you need to lose weight, continue to eat what you like, but reduce the amount you consume. Always leave at least one bite on the plate, and eat, say, 10% less than you are used to. Cut back on sweets and fried foods. Don't restrict yourself so much that you react by binging, but enough to encourage you a week from now when you measure your waist line. Start taking a good multi-vitamin, and reduce any consumption of alcohol and caffeinated beverages.

Take a Walk

Second, get regular exercise. Again, don't try to accomplish so much that you have to break all your old habits and feel as though you're no longer enjoying life. But take a brisk walk every morning, and, if possible, every evening after dinner. Try to walk at least twenty minutes each day.

Take up a Sport

Third, if necessary, consult your doctor, and then take up a sport. Engage in something that will safely raise your temperature and respiration.

YOUR MIND

Get Enough Sleep

This will not only improve your body chemistry and strengthen your immune system, but it will make you mentally quicker and more effective on the job and in dealing with friends and family. If you're trying to get in as much living as possible before you die, perhaps you should realize that your current life style may actually be hastening your death.

Read

Read. At first, perhaps, you'll read a book or two about surviving terrorism. But once you have the rudiments, leave this topic behind and broaden your horizons by reading a good novel or a non-fiction book that will help develop your character, make you more efficient, more knowledgeable, or simply more interesting. And break the TV habit!

Take Up a Hobby

Learn something new. Build a cabinet, design a dress, plant a garden, paint a landscape, rebuild an automobile engine, create a model train set, take up piano, or study any of a thousand other things, some of which might supplement your salary or even replace your current job.

Develop New Skills

Use your newly acquired carpentry skills to install a HEPA filter system in your new family safe room. Use your new cooking skills to can foods for an emergency.

SPIRITUAL

It is in the realm of the unseen that the greatest work is done in your life.

This is the place which you can enter only through faith. Here you meet the unseen God who can cleanse your spirit, erase your guilt, bring peace to your life, and embolden you to attempt and accomplish things that are larger than you can imagine.

It is from this launch pad of faith that you will meet The One who reveals your sin, encourages you in righteousness, whispers soft cautions when you err, strengthens you to extend love in the face of hatred, brings peace and joy, and helps you to lead others to a place of strength.

Perhaps the spiritual should have been listed before the physical and the mental because, if you get the spiritual part right, then you will discover the strength and grace and wisdom to deal with the others.

Faith-Based Responses to Fear

For those who do not enjoy the peace of mind associated with a personal relationship with the Lord, the possibility of a terrorist attack is truly terrifying. Those individuals are more likely to suffer sleep deprivation and emotional stress from fear of loss. This includes the loss of life, loss of loved ones, loss of possessions, and the loss of personal influence, wealth and power.

The scriptures—both the Old and New Testaments— have much to say about fear in the life of the believer.

Principal among these passages is Hebrews 13:6: "So that we may boldly say, The Lord is my helper, and I will not fear what man shall do unto me."

We who have received Jesus as our Savior have also received him as our Lord, our King and our Protector. We are not to fear what humans may do to harm us.

Yet, we are to fear some things. We are to fear God and what God can do to us if we persist in our sin born of unbelief. "Happy is the man that feareth always: but he that hardeneth his heart shall fall into mischief" (Prov 28:14).

The great truth here is that when we come into fellowship with God through a personal relationship with his Son, Jesus Christ, we receive a clear conscience. We are freed from the burden and consequences of sin and guilt, and from all earthly fears.

For, "In righteousness you will be established; you will have nothing to fear. Terror will be far removed; it will not come near you. (Isa 54:14, NIV). As John tells us, "There is no fear in love; but perfect love casteth out fear; because fear hath torment. He that feareth is not made perfect in love" (I John 4:18).

Consider how Daniel's three friends responded to King Nebuchadnezzar: "If it be so, our God whom we serve is able to deliver us from the burning fiery furnace, and he will deliver us out of thine hand, O King. (Dan 3:17).

The purpose of terrorism is to terrorize. And while the vicious acts of a terrorist may harm and even kill you, the terror of the terrorist's acts need not touch you. While you may physically "perish," yet you shall live forever. Once you are a child of God, you may be as calm as the eagle hovering over her young in a nest on the edge of a great Niagara.

Jesus said, "My peace I give you." Picture the Son of God, who suffered the horrors of the cross, now resurrected and standing at the right hand of God, ever living to bring you the peace that he promised, the peace that passes understanding.

You may make peace with God

We want peace in the world. But there can be no peace in the world until each of us makes peace with God. We can't be at peace with ourselves or with one another until we are at peace with God.

Whatever your challenge—a terrible self image, a problem with your weight, trials at work, difficulty getting along with your mate or your children, or a shameful habit that you cannot break—it is from this faith that you will draw the grace and power to overcome.

Examine the following verses from the Bible:

Romans 3:23; Romans 6:23; Romans 5:8; Romans 10: 9,10.

If you're not certain how their words might apply to you, start contacting preachers in your area until you find one who joyfully and confidently explains from the scriptures how your faith in Jesus Christ will give you peace with God.

Remember, after you make peace with God, you need not fear the consequences of a terrorist attack or any natural disaster. You will be free, now and forever. And you will be a member of the family of faith, free to fellowship and rely upon one another for encouragement and assistance.

18. Prepare Your Family

OUR MOST PRECIOUS TRUST

Your children are your most precious trust. Their survival justifies substantial labor and investment on your part.

In September, 2004, we listened in horror to the news that troops in Chechnya had made a futile effort to negotiate the release of over a 1,000 children and adults from a local school. During the standoff, a bomb was exploded in the crowded school auditorium killing many. Then hundreds panicked, and more children were massacred as they attempted to escape their captors, with many of them shot in the back.

Later, as survivors were carried out of the building, we were exposed to photos of nearly naked children who had suffered from excessive heat while crowded together in the gymnasium. They were suffering from dehydration, hunger, exhaustion and shock.

If the school officials or parents been more alert, they might have discovered the cache of weapons that had been hidden in the school at an earlier date by the terrorists. Perhaps authorities could have frustrated the scheme. Had the victims been better prepared, more of them might have survived.

These failures point up the importance of your always being alert for the unusual, and immediately reporting anything suspicious to authorities.

Equally important, that terrorist attack on students and their families should have brought home to all of us the potential for a similar attack on our own soil.

Since our police and intelligence people cannot be everywhere, we need to ask ourselves, "What steps can we take to help protect our children?"

How may we influence our school systems to take these danger more seriously? What steps can we suggest they take that will not overburden their already overworked staffs and underweight budgets? After all, the lives of our teachers and educational personnel are also at risk. Perhaps most importantly, what can we teach our children about how to respond to such an assault, and what can we provide them that might improve their chances of survival?

Both FEMA and the Red Cross provide excellent materials designed to help our children prepare for terror, but their emphasis is generally on the psychological impact.

That is certainly a valid concern, but comforting our children will not make the danger go away. No matter how tenuous, they will be more hopeful if we provide them with some guidelines for dealing with such situations.

Help Your Child Deal with Terror

Children have a certain innate heroism about them. Perhaps it is simply foolhardiness based on ignorance, but it also demonstrates a touching innocence and honesty. Many children would offer themselves as a sacrifice for others. Not knowing much about pain and death, children do not share an adult's fear. In contrast, adults are afraid that their children will suffer trauma from living in a prolonged state of fear. They worry that their children will not be able to handle the incessant stress and anxiety. Happily, in most cases children can handle it more handily than adults. Often, children pick up their anxiety from parents.

It is comical to hear psychologists speak of children being stressed and traumatized by discussions about or preparations for terror or warfare. This is true in some cases, but certainly not in all.

Adults might be surprised to learn that their children often deal with stress much better than they do. Our real concern should be whether our children are receiving the best possible preparation to survive a terrorist attack, because that training will reduce their fears. Ignorance often breeds fear.

Children live for the moment, and can scarcely wait for tomorrow. If we decide to equip them against terrorism, we should make our instructions and our preparations as simple and matter a fact as we do when we prepare their daily school lunch or ride herd on their homework assignments. It should become a necessary and even boring part of their daily regimen.

Do you want your children to continue at a level of ignorance that might result in the loss of their lives? Of course you don't! You want to bolster them in a positive manner. One of the things we all want for our children is to reduce the everyday stress that surrounds them. We certainly don't want them to grow up with the "eat, drink and be merry because tomorrow we die" syndrome that many of us experienced during the height of the Cold War.

When you carefully prepare your family, they no longer carry unnecessary stress around with them. Careful preparation increases confidence and reduces stress.

Initially perhaps, when you're discussing these preparations with your children, they may become upset. It's very important that you exude confidence. And remember, you may explain the "how" to your children without telling them the "why."

Keep this in mind. The stress that may be connected with these preparations is not a lot different from the stress involved in teaching your children how to avoid sexual predators and kidnappers, or how to escape the seduction of illicit drugs, alcohol and tobacco. They must learn at the earliest age that there is both good and evil in the world, and they must also learn that it is necessary to stand as firmly for the first as they stand against the latter. Never forget that they learn best by watching the example that you, their parent, sets.

Terrorism is a fact of life that our children must be just as prepared to resist as they are prepared to resist sexual deviants and drug pushers.

Of course, we can't prepare for every eventuality. We can't build giant structures over our schools to protect them from the obscure danger of a crashing jet liner. We must recognize that there are moments in time when we all come to the end of ourselves, when we must rely on someone greater that we are to protect us and watch over our children. Our children need to understand this as well. But, we must also help equip and train them to protect and fend for themselves—physically, mentally and spiritually.

Once you've taught your child some of the things that they need to know to respond to an emergency, you won't have to continually rehash it, though you may want to refresh them on a monthly basis. Repetition is important. But you can count on vital details being recalled as they are needed.

Most important, however, is that they learn to keep their survival packs close at hand, and that they know when and how to use each carefully packaged item. It's your job to make certain that items such as food, water and flashlight batteries are kept fresh and updated. Some day you may be very glad that you taught them these rudiments of survival and that you equipped them for the real world.

Your child may be an adorable "little lamb." What you don't want is for your child to become a sheep on the way to slaughter. You don't want them following blindly behind some ignorant and unequipped person who may lead them into trouble rather than away from it. It is very important that your child knows how to react in as many situations as possible. You may be concerned that preparing for potential disaster may frighten your children. But your children know that this is a dangerous world. They know about 9/11 and Columbine and kidnapping and murder and terrorism and war and rumors of war and earthquakes and pestilence and distress of nations.

Your children will be comforted by the fact that you are doing your job as a parent. They will see that you are carefully and confidently preparing to protect them from harm. They'll follow you. Children are adventurers.

Talk to Your Child about Terrorism and Disasters

When facing any kind of emergency, you need to have a positive mental attitude. One of the finest illustrations of this attitude is seen in the lead character in the motion picture, "Life Is Beautiful." This Jewish man, with his small son, are herded into a Nazi death camp. This father brings humor in the midst of deprivation, exudes confidence in the face of horror, and somehow girds his son for the worst possible outcome. Oh that each of us could have such a brilliant and optimistic outlook!

RESOURCES

FEMA RESOURCES

FEMA provides a wealth of information to help parents and concerned adults prepare children for terrorist attacks. But their recommendations do not deal with anything approaching the scenario of the school takeover in Chechnya.

The help that FEMA currently offers, however, is invaluable. Visit http://www.fema.gov, and click the "FEMA for Kids" link. Here, the children are introduced to "Herman the Crab" who, among other things, will share with them his search for a disaster proof shell, and informs the kids that, "Disasters aren't fun, but learning about them is."

And that's the tact that you should take. "Disasters aren't fun, but learning about them is."

FEMA's Children's Page

The Children's page on FEMA's website provides six things that they want children to rembember. (This advice is pretty good for parents, too!)

"Disasters can happen. They often happen quickly and without warning, and they can be scary for you and your parents. For example, you may have to leave your home and you may not be able to go to school. You may not be able to sleep in your own bed and things may be confusing for a while. There are SIX important things to remember:

"Disasters don't last very long. Soon, things will be back to normal.

"You can get a new routine if you can't go home for awhile. You will settle down into a new place and you will meet new friends.

"Look to your parents or other adults for help when you feel scared or confused. They will help you understand what is happening. Don't be afraid to ask questions like:

"How long will we be in the shelter?

"When will I go back to school?

"Sometimes it helps to write about your experiences or to draw pictures about what has happened. You can describe what happened and how you feel. The FEMA for Kids Web site can post your projects.

"It's OK to cry during a disaster, but remember, things will GET BETTER.

"You may be able to help out. Children of all ages can help in the shelter by baby sitting other children or cleaning up or serving food. You can even help with sandbagging or cleaning up your house after a tornado or hurricane or earthquake."

FEMA's Course for Children

According to FEMA, the course was developed to help children cope in uncertain times. The curriculum is arranged in three chapters:

Chapter 1: "Feelings," includes lessons and activities dealing with feelings of loss, sadness and anger.

Chapter 2: "Facts and Perspectives," provides information on how to discern facts as reported by the media, yet not continue to frighten children.

Chapter 3: "Future," provides positive ways for children and their families to respond to past events and plan for future uncertain times.

Red Cross Assistance

The Education and Training page on the FEMA website directs you to the Red Cross website for advice on how to help your child face fear. It contains advice for parents and guardians.

Facing Fear: Helping Young People Deal With Terrorism and Other Tragic Events http://www.redcross.org/disaster/masters/facingfear/.

The pamphlet, "Facing Fear" is available in printed form from your local American Red Cross chapter. To find your chapter, visit http://www.redcross.org/.

WHEN YOUR CHILDREN'S AGES VARY

Infant Children

Infants require unique care in the face of terrorism. Yet, in many ways, they are easier to care for than older children. If you have a nursing baby, then you need to provide for your own and your baby's hygiene, and provide yourself with plenty of fluids and healthy foods so that you can in turn care for your baby. If your baby is bottle fed, then you should keep formula and extra bottles in an emergency carry pack. All parents of infants should carry items like sanitary wipes, disposable diapers, changes of clothing, toys, and appropriate medicines.

If your infant is older, you will need to keep canned baby food on hand, plus disposable diapers, a change of clothes, and any necessary medications. Remember, your baby may be nursing today, but in a few months, she may be starting solid foods. You need to think in terms of storing jars of baby food now. And keep diapers on hand for any child that is not potty trained.

After age 3, it is assumed that the child will need the same sorts of items as you, food, water, clothing, etc. If you must leave your toddler in day care or with a friend or relative, make clear to them what you want them to do with your child in the event of any emergency.

In all cases, you should have face masks and other emergency equipment that you have learned to adapt to their smaller heads and bodies.

All children need books and toys that are compact and easily transported. But toys aren't enough. They will need your continual comfort and love.

School Age Children

During the school year, your child is away from home up to ten hours each weekday. What you teach them, and the items that you send them off to school with, could well mean the difference between life and death.

College Age and Working Teens

We see little of, and have less influence over, our high school and college age children. We can and should express our concerns about their welfare and offer to help them create their own emergency survival packs. If they still live at home, we should attempt to incorporate them into our disaster planning and assign them significant responsibilities.

EMERGENCY DRILLS

Home Emergency Drills

An attack may come at anytime, and catch you while you are away from home, at church, school, work, shopping, or traveling. Try to avoid being blind-sided by such an attack by imagining in advance what might occur in a given place. Imagine how you and your children should respond, and what resources will be required. Then discuss the scenario with your family and perhaps even drill them in their responses. You will be amazed at the incites and observations your children offer.

Your local fire department frequently warns you to change the batteries in your smoke detectors, to plan emergency exit routes from your home, and to conduct family fire drills.

While you are conducting home fire drills, you should also drill for other kinds of emergencies, such as an attack with WMDs. Ask yourself, what each member of the family should do when they learn of such an attack, regardless of the time of day. How should you respond? Where should you go?

School Emergency Drills

We are all aware that emergencies may occur while our children are at school. We have little control over how these emergencies will be handled, but we can express our concern to our school officials by stating them at PTF meetings and by writing the administrators.

A school emergency may consist of any of a variety of situations including student or staff violence, a loss of electrical power, a fire, earthquake, tornado, ice storm, or a terrorist attack. Every school in America should conduct emergency drills that cover as many scenarios as possible.

Fire Drills

In most places, laws require schools to conduct periodic fire drills. The children learn that no matter where they are in the building, they have certain responsibilities. They learn to carry out those responsibilities quietly and seriously. Some are assigned the responsibility for closing any open windows and doors, or to turn out lights. Others get on line and march quietly, by a prescribed rout, from the building. Sometimes the older students are to take responsibility for the younger, or the strong for those who are disabled. Outside the building, teachers call role, and all children and staff are accounted for. There is never fear nor hysteria. When a fire actually breaks out in a school, everyone exits the building nearly as quietly and with as little concern as during the practice drills.

When tornadoes threaten, many schools move children toward the center of the building, or to the basement areas, away from windows where they are shielded by the most solid walls. All schools move the students and staff out of the structure if there is a fire. Many schools lock down their facilities if there is a report of an unstable and threatening individual in the area. During the early 1940s and 50s, students were moved to inside hallways and lower floors for air raid drills.

When your children attend school, they are under the protection and authority of the school's administration. There may come a time or circumstance where the administration no longer has control of a situation. In that event, you need to have given your children instructions on how they should conduct themselves.

Family Emergency Drills

Teach your children when and how to don emergency gear, such as masks and goggles. Exhort them to remain calm and to obey school authorities. If school authorities become unable to function, teach your children how to take charge of their own lives. Encourage them to help anyone they can, and teach them when and why to evacuate an area.

Most importantly, help them to overcome any peer pressure that might mock their preparations. If they are the only ones equipped with goggles when an incident occurs, they may also be the only ones who can see through blinding fumes to guide their fellow students from a burning building.

Parental Instruction

Similar at home rehearsals are invaluable in preparing each of us for everything from an early morning house fire, to a terrorist attack, or tornado.

You must prayerfully decide what scenarios to discuss with your children, and you must decide how you would have them conduct themselves under various circumstances. Keep in mind that many children are more resilient than adults. They tend to be idealistic, adventuresome and bold. Yes, they are apt to be impulsive and foolish, but their very impulsiveness and determination are characteristics that could save their lives.

There is more than one reason that we don't send middle-aged men into combat. The first, of course, is because they are not in adequate physical condition. But as we grow older, we not only grow soft. We also tend to become more conservative and careful. We lack the fire and the courage of youth. Many middle-aged men would die in combat because they would be afraid to make snap decisions or to take risks. Being young has its advantages.

Give your children the best advice you can, then leave the outcome to God. If you fail to give them what they need—advice, survival items, or a godly foundation—what will the result be?

TRAINING FOR VARIOUS SITUATIONS

Fire

You are in greater risk of dying from smoke or fire than from a WMD. Fire may not seem to represent as great a danger, but remember that the World Trade Center buildings did not collapse immediately after being struck by those enormous jet liners. It was the intense heat, generated by the thousands of gallons of jet fuel, that weakened the supporting columns and caused each tower to "pancake."

Having reminded you of these horrific scenes of terror, you may feel that your best efforts will be futile in attempting to prepare yourself and your child for survival. Nothing could be further from the truth. The Boy Scouts of America have a simple two-word motto: "Be prepared." Your preparation—mental, physical and material—is the key to confidence and the means to victory.

The Enemy Within

The situation changes once terrorists actually begin to enter a building with the intent of taking hostages. For those who are quick-witted and courageous, there may be an opportunity to drift into an unoccupied hallway and escape.

The first principal of escape holds that a person must attempt to do so as soon as possible, before the enemy has solidified his hold and before the victims have become psychological captives.

Consider the Chechnyan school standoff. Once the invaders had rigged their bombs and positioned their people to cover the hostages as well all doors and windows in the school, the situation was pretty much hopeless. When the children became thoroughly cowed by their menacing captors, they necessarily acquiesced to their commands. They became enervated from heat exhaustion and lack of fluids, and were incapable of thought or action. They became psychologically and physically unequipped to make an escape attempt. Ultimately, hundreds died.

To suggest that a child might risk his life to escape in such a situation is, of course, controversial. Many will prefer to encourage their children to acquiesce to the terrorists, to be quiet, cooperative and obedient. And that might well result in their survival. But it didn't help hundreds of children in Chechnya because the terrorists massacred them at the first sign that their control was slipping. And it most assuredly doesn't work where a child is kidnapped by a sexual predator or serial killer. Consider encouraging them to try to escape at the earliest opportunity, to slip away repeatedly. Never let them submit mentally. Instruct them to always be looking for a possibility of escape.

Bomb Threats and Explosions

Imagine that there is an explosion in or near your child's school, and that, although the children are uninjured, they may be blinded by choking dust and suffer from ringing and pain in their ears. This could result in disorientation, confusion and panic. All too quickly they could run further into harm's way or collapse in shock.

You can limit some of these possibilities by describing or even role playing hypothetical situations with your children. Try to describe what might happen around them, discuss how those events might make them feel, and talk with them about how they might respond. If they are properly drilled, their responses in such a situation will be more measured and thoughtful. The unknown often brings fear. Preparation is the foundation for confidence and for survival. It is very important that you assure them that it is proper to take measured responses in the event of an emergency.

It's unlikely that your children will be forewarned of a possible bombing. They may not even be aware of a nearby detonation. Nonetheless, they need to be prepared. All of us like to believe that we are very poised and steady in the face of disaster, but the truth is that most of us are shocked by such an occurrence, and find ourselves without the ability to act. Those who have been trained to handle emergencies, and have been through the horror of warfare, firefighting or policework, are better able to focus on the job at hand.

The first thing boys and girls should be taught to do in the event of an imminent attack depends upon the estimated time available. Can they flee the area? If not, they should be moved as far away from the area of danger as possible and told to duck and cover. If they have a Pocket Pack, they should put their nuisance dust masks over their mouths and noses to mask themselves from pollution and biological hazards. Next, they should put on their goggles so that their eyes will not damaged by chemicals or pollutants in the air. They can wrap the aluminized space blankets about themselves to protect themselves from flash burns. You and your children need to learn to protect yourselves from the dangers of flying and broken glass, smoke, fire, deadly gases, and broken electrical cables.

Along with these come the attendant risks of wounds, poisoning, electrocution, fire, and even structural collapse. These are dangers that might result not only from terrorist attacks, but also during and after tornadoes, hurricanes, and earthquakes. The training and equipment that you provide your children to survive natural disasters will also help them survive and recover from terrorist attacks, including biological, chemical and radiatiological agents.

You may feel overwhelmed by the mere prospect of you or your child being caught up in a terrorist attack. Keep in mind, however, that your feelings will not stop such an attack. In fact, the resulting spiritual malaise may encourage terrorists to believe that such an attack will be more profitable. Preparation is a means of fighting back and of preventing attacks. What's more, the preparation and alertness of you, your children, and millions of others like you, may deter or foil such an attack.

WMDs

If there is danger of radiation, children should immediately take the prescribed dosage of potassium iodide, swallowing the tablet with some of the bottled water or fruit juice they carry in their emergency pack. If they are not wearing their surgical mask, goggles and aluminized blanket, they should put them on. Then they need to find a masonry building with structural integrity where they can hide themselves away from the source of radiation, either in a central room on a lower floor or, better yet, in a basement. Instruct them to stay away from windows and doors, and to sit with their backs against a supporting wall. Unless there are high winds blowing radioactive dust about, they should leave doors open wide enough that, if a roof collapses, they may still be able to escape the room where they are sheltering.

In almost all circumstances surrounding a terrorist attack— whether explosion, fire, radiation, biological or chemical incident—a surgical mask will help offset many of the dangers (except for chemical gasses). It will decrease the risk of heart and lung disorders that result from dangerous dust in the air. Certainly it's useful in preventing inhalation of anthrax and other biological agents, and in preventing asthma attacks.

A gas mask, such as the people of Israel carry during high alerts, is of course, much better. In the case of Ricin, the chemical agent used by terrorists a few years ago to kill people at a Tokyo subway station, people needed to have gas masks and impregnable fabric covering their entire bodies.

That's why, in the event of a chemical attack, if you see victims collapsing some distance away, you should flee in the opposite direction. If you or your children see anyone attacked with some sort of nerve gas or biological agent, you should move away and notify emergency personnel. These victims must only be approached by trained emergency personnel wearing special gear and possessing unique training. If you attempt to help them, you do so at risk of your own life. In most cases, children are not strong enough to help adults; their first responsibility is to get themselves and other small children out of the area.

TEACH CHILDREN TO RESPOND

Teach Them to Identify the Threats

As soon as possible, the children should be guided away from the vicinity and kept under the care of responsible adults until transported to their homes or an alternate shelter. If a teacher or another adult is at hand, they should take instructions from her. Lacking the guidance of a trained adult, the children should prepare to muster everyone in the area and file quietly away from the scene of destruction. They should avoid crowds, for crowds constitute an additional target. If no adults are available to provide guidance, your children should have sufficient understanding as whether to shelter in place or start for a prearranged rendezvous.

Once you have learned how to identify potential threats, such as biological, chemical or nuclear radiation, you need to teach your child how to identify and respond to them. Keep it simple. Teach your children whether to flee or to seek shelter. Teach them where to flee and what kind of shelter to look for. Discuss places where they could shelter in place, such as their school, or substantial structures that they would pass en route home. Help them understand what kind of structure offers the best chances of survival.

Teach Them the "Buddy System"

Just as in swim safety, school, administrators should make children responsible for one another using a "buddy system." This assures that two specific children take responsibility for one another. They constantly monitor one another's whereabouts, and become "buddies" when things might turn bad. Children should be offered first choice over whom they'd like to buddy up with. The buddie system provides them with someone to talk to, to share their fears, test their ideas, and encourage one another. "One is good, but two are better."

Upon exiting the danger zone, each set of buddies should examine one another for bruises or wounds. A gaping wound is of course far more life threatening than is a broken bone. Loss of blood is dangerous, and open wounds constitute a place of access for contaminants. Anything that appears serious should immediately be brought to the attention of a responsible adult. If no adult is available, the children should attempt to wash open wounds with the cleanest water available, then bind them up.

What can you do to prepare your child for survival? What can you teach her? What can you put in his survival pack? Most children are already overloaded with books, musical instruments, sporting goods and school supplies. Indeed, most school administrators limit children from carrying many objects that they consider potential weapons. So, what can you provide them that has little bulk or weight, will pass the school's muster, and will be useful to them in the event of a terror attack?

ALTERNATIVES

You are faced with some alternatives here, depending on the answers to two questions. First, do school regulations prohibit your child carrying any of the suggested items, and, if so, can you get the authorities to alter those rules? Second, how much weight and bulk is your child now carrying to school, and how much is he or she capable of carrying without discomfort or injury?

Children need basically the same things that you need in your pack. Assuming that your child is small and limited to a very small package, consider the Pocket Pack described in Chapter 8. Keep in mind, however, that schools are subject to lock downs, so you may want to add at least a small bottle of water and an energy bar to help them through long periods of waiting.

The next step up is the Fannie Pack described in Chapter 9. This is followed by the Day Pack, described In chapter 10. It is unlikely that children could manage the Day Pack because they are probably already carrying a back pack containing books, lunch, gym clothes, and other items. It might be possible to put the contents of a Fannie Pack into a small lunch box and store it in the bottom of the day pack they are already carrying.

The Day Pack is designed for all sorts of emergencies. It contains communications equipment, breathing apparatus, food and water, first aid supplies, and other items. Not all of these items will be of use to everyone in all situations, but some of them may.

If there is a lock down at your child's high school, and he or she must remain inside for a day or two, this will provide some food, water and other comforts to each child who carries it.

The items listed here may be disputed, but we can show how, under various circumstances, they can make the difference on the one hand, between life and death, and on the other, between comfort and discomfort.

The items that you will gather and store in your child's Day Pack could prove to save lives or provide comfort in many situations. Something as simple as an aspirin tablet, administered to a person experiencing a heart attack or stroke can save his life. That help is only possible, of course, if you have packed that aspirin tablet, along with some water to wash it down, and have the presence of mind to administer it.

As you read this book, you are achieving three things. First, you are identifying potential dangers and how you might respond to them. Second, you are learning how to survive, and, hopefully, preparing to weather the storms of adversity. Finally, you are gaining confidence that you are as prepared as possible, and more prepared than most, to survive.

Foreknowledge of what you need to do in an emergency, and the confidence born of your preparation, will help you to remain calm and to communicate that spirit to those around you. You must stay as calm as possible so that you can help others and also to keep your mind uncluttered as you strive to recognize things around you that might be useful in promoting survival.

If you tend to be negative, read a few of the histories of survivors down through the centuries to learn that the most important survival item is not found in a "survival pack." The most important item is your will to survive.

19. Self Defense

As a civilian, your first responsibility is the preservation of your life and that of your loved ones.

Most of us want to avoid confrontation. We want to avoid injury to ourselves, but we also don't want to harm others. For over two centuries, people of other countries have misinterpreted America's good nature and sense of fair play as a sign of weakness. Until we started facing terrorist "rats" that crawl out of the slime to kill innocent people, whom we never unilaterally attacked.

But our enemies mistake our good nature for weakness. We have never been weak. Check your history books. We not only defeated the greatest military powers in two wars, but we pulled our ally's chestnuts out of the fire while we did it. Then, after World War II, we spent billions in Marshall Aid to rebuild the Europe we had just conquered. And, as soon as possible, we withdrew our troops. No, we Americans aren't soft. We're simply moral.

SEEK ASSISTANCE

In most cases, Americans whose lives or property are endangered are able to call on the police or fire departments in their own communities for assistance. This will be a less likely possibility in time of a terrorist attack. When we are left to our own devices because emergency authorities are too busy to help us, we tend either to flee or fight back.

Our enemy strives to remain unseen. His goal is to destroy people like you and me–thousands of us if he can—then run away to attack again another day. If a terrorist strikes in your vicinity, you may have to flee, just as you would from a hurricane. If you find someone in your path who intends to harm you or your loved ones, you may also have to oppose them with physical force.

Who are the evil people who might block your path? First, of course, there are the terrorists. Their goal is to do damage far out of proportion to their numbers. The battle against them is essentially one being waged by our government. Apart from the terrorists, we regrettably have many within our own society who will exploit any emergency situation to loot vacant homes and businesses, and commit acts of senseless destruction and violence, including the raping of helpless women. When Hurricane Ivan hit Haiti, a prison was damaged, and scores of dangerous inmates escaped to wreak havoc on an already devastated population.

FLEE OR FIGHT

This is your opportunity to help your family avoid such situations. While the legal issues are beyond the scope of this book, the moral and practical considerations are not.

You can take two approaches to protect yourself.

Flee from Danger

First, try to get away from areas of dangerous activity where there is a high potential for looting and physical attack. Try to remain near and to travel with, people who act in a responsible manner.

This is not cowardice. You may be willing, even eager, to fight evil. But you should not put your family at risk or demand that they suffer for your faith (or lack of faith). Get them out of harm's way; then decide what your role should be.

Both the Old and the New Testaments include numerous accounts of what is called the principal of fleeing. Prime examples in the Old Testament include Moses fleeing into the desert to escape the Pharaoh's wrath and David hiding from Saul in caves. In the New Testament, we read the account of Joseph taking Mary and the child Jesus down into Egypt to escape the murderous wrath of King Herod. Herod subsequently ordered the murder of all male babies in Bethlehem, hoping to kill the Christ child. Later, when Jesus' enemies would have murdered him, he was removed from their presence and appeared at another place, a divine and supernatural means of deliverance.

Defend Yourself and Your Loved Ones

Your other option is to be prepared to defend yourself and your family.

As a civilian, your responsibility is to help preserve the country that has provided you with the freedom to pursue life, liberty and happiness. So, if a time arises when our police, firefighters and military aren't able to carry the full load and the government has to call on ordinary people, as it did two centuries ago, it will be up to citizen soldiers like you and me to stand in the gap.

Up until now, a civilian's role has been as uncomplicated as keeping our senses alert to recognize possible terrorists and to report any suspicious activities to authorities.

Yet, thousands of courageous civilians have been putting themselves in harm's way through their service as full or part-time law-enforcement agents, medical personnel, fire fighters and members of the National Guard.

Others civilians have identified opportunities for service and dared to fight back. On 9/11, when passengers on Flight 93 learned that their plane might be used as a missile to attack Washington, they sacrificed their lives in order to stop the enemy. "Let's Roll!" became a rallying cry against the tyranny of terrorism.

In a future emergency situation, you might be called upon to fight fires, offer first aid, nurse the sick and wounded, dole out supplies, prepare meals, and assist or take the lead in any of a thousand other jobs. If you have done a proper job of preparing for your family's survival, you will be far better equipped mentally, physically and spiritually, to come to the aid of your country in the event of a natural disaster or a terrorist attack.

If, however, you have not done a proper job of preparation, you will become part of the problem rather than part of the solution. Your family may suffer and even perish because you didn't make the effort, and you will become a burden to society

THE CASE FOR SELF DEFENSE

The issue of self-defense is very controversial in America today. As little as fifty years ago, no court would question a man's right to shoot someone who threatened to burn his home or attack his family. All that has changed. Today, you may find yourself sued for not clearing your sidewalk of snow by the very thief who slips and falls while escaping with valuables he just stole from your house.

What will you do if your family is threatened? How will you react if your business is looted, your home is burned, or your teenage daughter is raped before your eyes? Will the rage that you feel at that future date turn into a sense of impotence, helplessness, and shame because you refused to prepare for such a possibility?

Do you have a moral right to defend your family against such attacks? If you don't know the answer to that question, than you are pitifully igno-

rant of the freedom you enjoy and the reasons your government was insti-
tuted. It's well past time that you should pick up some books and learn the
history of this, the greatest and most unique nation that has ever existed.

What does the Bible teach? What indeed would Jesus do? At no time
does the New Testament indicate that Jesus ever spoke out against capital
punishment or self-defense. Even when preparing to face his own illicit
judges, he never declared that the capital punishment that they would
mete out to him was otherwise illegal. Rather, he submitted himself to the
death on the cross because he was the perfect, final, sacrificial "lamb," who
had come into the world to die so that he could bear the sins of anyone and
everyone who would call upon his name.

Nor did he condemn the crucifixion of the men who hung upon either
side of him at Calvary. Rather, one of the criminals rebuked the other for
reviling Jesus, saying that Jesus was innocent, while they both deserved
their fate. The thief's final words were far more significant: "Lord, remember me when thou comest into thy kingdom." To which Jesus replied, "This
day shalt thou be with me in paradise."

Did Jesus ever refer to the issue of self-defense or the right to possess
deadly weapons? Absolutely? While he condemned those you use weapons
to murder others, he made it clear that individuals have the right to
defend themselves.

On the night in which he was betrayed, just before they left the upper
room to walk to the garden of Gesthemane, Jesus said, "'...if you don't have
a sword, sell your cloak and buy one. It is written: *And he was numbered
with the transgressors*, and I tell you that this must be fulfilled in me....'
The disciples said, 'See Lord, here are two swords.' 'That is enough,' he
replied" (Luke 22:36-38).

Subsequent passages indicate that Jesus wanted his disciples armed
to protect them from thieves and bandits, for he had to fulfill the scriptures. When one of his disciples attempted to defend them against consti-
tuted authority, Jesus condemned him for his actions. Luke's book
continues: "When Jesus' followers saw what was going to happen, they
said, 'Lord, should we strike with our swords?' And one of them struck the
servant of the high priest, cutting off his right ear. But Jesus answered,
'No more of this!' And he touched the man's ear and healed him" (Luke
22:49-51).

Jesus sanctioned the use of weapons in self-defense. In addition, the
founding fathers of the United States, like our first president, George
Washington, feared despotism and declared it the right and responsibility
of citizens to arm themselves to defend the security of a free state.

Would I hesitate to give my life to protect that of my children or
grandchildren? I don't think so, but it is important that we never tell our
potential enemies how deep our convictions go or what tests they might
apply in an effort to break us.

PREPARATION

Physical Conditioning

You should strive to reach and remain in good physical condition. Twenty minutes of brisk exercise every day, coupled with careful eating habits, will take care of the basics. You should follow these practices in order to achieve the healthiest, happiest life style, but it is imperative if you are to be at your best to help others. Remember, the body is the temple of the Holy Spirit, and although Paul commented that, "...bodily exercise profits little," it is obvious that he walked many thousands of miles and stayed fit in the work of his ministry.

When we keep ourselves in good physical condition, we also have a better mental attitude and a more positive outlook on life. We're happier. What's more, those around us are challenged and inspired by our lifestyle. Finally, we are better equipped to think on our feet, walk that extra mile, and carry that extra load. We do more in less time. Life becomes a great adventure.

Santiana said, "He who does not learn from history is doomed to repeat it." Look at your world. In many nations, well-educated people have been forced to flee their homes. Even now, tens of thousands in the Sudan have had to run for their lives. They are destitute, hungry, sick and frightened. During World War II, millions of people who formerly had good jobs, were forced out onto the highways, walking from place to place, looking for something to eat and a place to sleep. God grant that we do not face such a future in America. But remember this, the weak do not survive such challenges. You need to be strong to practice survival with soul. Don't be discouraged if you are sick or disabled. Cling to the God of this truth: "The joy of the Lord is my strength." He will see you through.

Many women today are enrolling in marshal arts courses so that they can defend themselves against sexual predators and other violent people. Given right motives—and controlling the urge to simply strike out at someone that we don't like—the marshal arts are worthy of consideration by people of both sexes and of all ages. If nothing else, they tone the body and focuses the mind. And you can learn the skills without embracing the eastern philosophy.

Mental and Spiritual Conditioning

These are not the same thing. Knowledge does not imply wisdom. Anger does not imply moral strength. You require knowledge to make wise decisions. You require moral fiber, and this is more of a spiritual matter than an ethical one.

Weapons Training

The issue of self-defense is fraught with implications of moral and legal significance. Certainly, it is a very personal issue. Controversy immediately arises when the issue of carrying weapons for self-defense is raised.

THE RIGHT TO KEEP AND BEAR ARMS...

The 2nd Amendment to the U.S. Constitution arose out of the realization that a benign government can become a dictatorial regime that is endemic to freedom. Thus, the founding fathers wrote, *A well regulated militia, being necessary to the security of a free state, the right of the people to keep and bear arms, shall not be infringed.*

This amendment reflects the historical reality that all our 18th Century American ancestors had to do was to show up at a place of muster with musket, powder and ball. Of course, any individual might also initiate that muster.

In terms of the effectiveness of the weapon that a man hung over his front door, the deadlier and more accurate, the better. Thus a the man carrying the far more advanced and accurate rifle was most prized among the recruits of the American War for Independence.

Firearms

If you do keep firearms, put them in a place where children (and thieves) cannot reach them. Make certain that you are trained in their use.

U.S. Caliber 30 M1 Carbine

Don't ever point the gun at someone unless you are certain that they are a serious danger to your or your loved ones. Always assume that all weapons are loaded and handle them accordingly. If you tell a threatening person to stop moving toward you, and they ignore you, be prepared to pull the trigger. Do not let them get within reach of you. If you cannot do that, you should not have the gun. They will take it from you and may use it to shoot you.

ALTERNATIVES

The following suggestions are based upon research. You may find these measures repugnant. Make certain that you are well persuaded in your own heart before undertaking action with any weapon.

Pepper Spray and Mace

These can neutralize an attacker and provide you an opportunity to escape. But they can also be fatal when used upon individuals with serious respiratory problems. It's imperative that you do not use any weapon until you are certain that the person confronting you is an imminent threat to your well being. Of course, you must not wait too long to make that determination.

The Taser

Consider investing in a Taser, the high voltage device that police use to temporarily paralyze a potentially violent person. Taser, the small company that produces stun guns for police agencies, recently saw their stock jump 20% in one day after they introduced a "Taser" for civilian use. It is gaining in popularity because it can be used to disable a home invader, yet it does not present the same danger to children that a firearm might represent. Since you will not risk wounding your attacker, you will be less reluctant to shock him. Once you have disabled the person, you can bind his wrists behind him using a couple of plastic wire loops, similar to the twists used by electricians to bundle wires. Even in "peace time," a Taser is an excellent device to have with you when you are out on the streets alone, walking, cycling or jogging.

As an aside, a Taser can also be used to counteract the venom of poisonous snakes, scorpions and spiders. A missionary for Wycliffe Bible Translators related that high-voltage, low-amperage electrical shock is the safest, most certain way to neutralize both hemotoxic and neurotoxic poisons. The electrical current, immediately applied over the bite marks, will break down the complex proteins of which the poisons are composed. It works equally well with all snake and insect bites. With larger amounts of venom, or more deadly venoms, the shock may have to be applied several times during the first hour. The missionary even related how an automobile electrical coil can be used to apply high-voltage shock to a venomous bite to break down the poison.

Knives, and clubs.

These weapons may be used for self-defense, but unless you are trained and skilled in their use, you are more apt to have them taken from you and used against you. Truck stops used to sell a variety of flexible "clubs" designed for the driver's self defense.

CONTRIVED WEAPONS

These weapon can be "manufactured" in seconds by victims in hostage situations who realize that their lives will be forfeit if they do not take action, and who are determined to foil the terrorist's plans and overcome their would-be assassins.

These extreme measures may appear futile against trained terrorists using conventional firearms, but a group of determined people, who realize that their lives are probably forfeit, might be able to disrupt the plans of fanatics armed with contrived weapons like box knives.

Remember, there may be three or four terrorists on a jetliner, but it's becoming more difficult for those terrorists to smuggle on board guns, knives and explosives. If the passengers rise up as one—and this is the key—they should be able to subdue or kill their terrorist assailants.

If the passengers in two or three seats on each side of an aisle are able to attack a terrorist as he walks by, they may be able to blind, bruise, or even kill them as they drag them to the floor of the plane.

If not, they are in much the same situation as the passengers on Flight 93. They may ultimately and heroically give their lives to stop the terrorists, thus foiling their attempt to use the aircraft against a major target such as The White House or the Pentagon.

Newspapers and Magazines

A magazine or newspaper may be rolled into a tight conical shape with the resulting hard and sharp point becoming an excellent weapon for use at close quarters. Wrap your hand securely around the center of the pointed cylinder and try to drive the point into the terrorist's soft body tissue. Aim for the Adam's Apple, the solar plexus, the kidneys or the groin. If you have any kind of tape available, you may wrap it around the cylinder just behind the point and also around the center and wide end of the roll to help maintain its tightness and shape. The trick is to alert other able and willing passengers to your intentions. Even if the terrorists insist that all hostages remain in their seats and put their heads down on their knees, many passengers could surreptitiously prepare these weapons and bring them to bear at some whispered or shouted signal.

Leather Belt with a Metal Buckle

If you own a leather belt with a metal buckle, fold it in half and wrap the folded part around one hand, so that the buckle becomes a dangerous flailing tool when swung at the eyes and hands of terrorists.

A Set of Keys

Wrap the bulk of your keys or key case in a handkerchief, paper napkin, or wad of tissues, grip it firmly in the palm of your hand, leaving two or three keys protruding between your fingers, and use this contrived weapon to punch at your assailant's eyes and face.

Hair Spray, diluted ammonia, and other Chemicals

At this time, it's pretty well impossible to bring any chemicals on board a plane that might be used as a weapon. When you find yourself in another environment, you might use hair spray, diluted ammonia, pepper spray, or other chemicals to temporarily blind and disable an attacker.

RESTRAINING A DISARMED ATTACKER

Silk Scarf, Laptop Computer, Camera, and Headset Cords

These items will serve as devices for tying someone's hands.

Duct Tape

Duct tape is an effective means of binding wrists, elbows, knees and ankles, and can be used to cover someone's mouth to serve as a gag.

Wire Ties

Every electronics store sells wire ties—strong plastic strips of varying lengths—that you may use to bind the wrists and ankles of a potentially dangerous individual once he is subdued.

"NO GREATER LOVE...."

The first person to oppose the terrorists knows that he or she is likely to be injured or killed by them. If a sufficient number of people do not have the courage to attack simultaneously, that first person knows that he will sacrifice himself in an attempt to save the other hostages. This is heroism on the highest order. Jesus said, "No greater love has any man than this, that he lay down his life for another."

The terrorists, on the other hand, lay down their lives to murder others. They do so because they have been deceived. They have been told that they are creating a better world by spreading their failed philosophy, including their pathetic economic and educational concepts. And they are told that after they sacrifice themselves to kill others, they will immediately enter into a paradise where they will have their pick of beautiful virgins and a glorious afterlife. They are deluded. "He that lives by the sword shall die by the sword."

But the courageous individual who risks all to stop him may be laying down his life to protect the lives of others. There is no higher sacrifice.

CONCLUSION

If most passengers on an aircraft prepare themselves with one or more of these contrived weapons, and they have determined if necessary to offer their lives, they can bring down the terrorists. Committed people who know that their lives are on the line can foil a highjacking.

The very moment that it becomes clear that terrorists are trying to make hostages of people, the victims should take action. Instantly! They should not wait until the terrorists have control of the situation. They must rise up and act fearlessly, having long since determined in their hearts and minds that the terrorists are intent upon sacrificing their own lives to kill the them and probably to accomplish a much greater evil.

The terrorists will attempt to cow all hostages immediately. A favorite tactic is to immediately select a victim arbitrarily and brutally murder him or her. They might cast a man in a wheel chair over the side of a ship or cut a flight attendant's throat. This is raw terror and it generally works.

But now the terrorists know that an unsuspecting, surprised and shocked group of Americans were able to rally and respond heroically to foil their plans on Flight 93. Once the terrorists realize that most Americans have determined to give their lives in order to stop them, rather than go like sheep to their own slaughter, the terrorists will be less apt to attempt a high-jackings.

It's an easy resolution for us to make, for we know that if we don't fight back, we will die anyway. What did Ben Franklin say? Something like, "If we don't all hang together, we will all surely hang separately."

The terrorists may try to use these same weapons against you. But if you are courageous, if you decide that you are willing to sacrifice your life for the sake of others, there is a chance that all will survive.

Warning. The laws of your state and community may be interpreted against you in the exercise of your right to self defense. Make certain that you do not go beyond reasonable actions in defending yourself and your family.

If you do not prepare, you will relinquish the options to either flee or defend yourself. You will be forced to submit to anyone who chooses to abuse you or your loved ones. Take charge of your life or someone else will.

Appendix A: Food Inventory List

Table 1: Suggested Foods for Storage

Items per package	Size, weight or volume	Description	Number needed	Less, number on hand	Equals, number to buy	Store price	Total cost
1	46 oz	Apple Juice				$1.59	
1	7 oz	Apricots, dried				$2.89	
1	15 oz	Baked beans				$.98	
7	1.2 oz	Breakfast Bars				$3.50	
1	Can	Potato chips				$1.40	
4	6 oz can	Tuna, canned				$1.40	
3	6 oz can	Chicken, canned				$1.50	
1	Can	Vegetable				$.89	
1	Carton	Cereal				$2.00	
1	Pint	Cheese spread				$1.98	
12	Pack	Cookies				$5.20	
1	Can	Chunky soup, canned				$1.99	
1	32 oz	Lemonade mix*				$2.99	

1	package	Rice, flavored				$.79	
4	bottles	Frappucino				$5.00	
1	15 oz	Fruit cocktail, canned				$.75	
12	12 oz	Ginger ale				$2.50	
1	46 oz	Grape juice				$2 .79	
1	Jar	Coffee, instant				$3.59	
2	Cups	Jello cups				$1.00	
8	packages	Lance crackers				$1.84	
1	11.5 oz	Mixed nuts (unsalted)				$2.00	
1	package	Muffin mix*				$.71	
1	100 count	Multi-vitamin with Zinc				$5.00	
8	packages	Cereal bars				$3.44	
7	1.2 oz	Nutrition bar				$3.50	
1	46 oz	Orange juice, canned				$1.29	
1	15 oz	Peaches, canned				$1.09	
7	1.38 oz	Peanut butter crackers†				$1.75	
1	pint	Peanut Butter				$1.98	
1	46 oz	Pineapple juice, canned				$1.99	
6	12 oz	Powerade				$3.30	
2	cups	Pudding cups				$1.20	

12	individual	Oatmeal packets*				$3.39	
1	12 oz	Raisins				$2.49	
1	carton	Crackers, unsalted				$2.00	
1	15 oz	Soups*				$1.00	
1	16 oz	Spaghetti*				$$.79	
1	32 oz	Spaghetti sauce				$1.39	
1	15 oz	Ravioli				$1.59	
1	can	Spam				$1.59	
1	15 oz	Stew, chicken or beef				$1.95	
1	package	Stuffing mix*				$1.24	
1	4 lb.	Sugar				$1.40	
8	packs	Sugarless gum				$1.92	
10	packs	Hot chocolate mix*				$1.89	
48	bags	Tea				$2.99	
1	4 oz	Tuna or salmon pack				$2.10	
1	3.5 oz	Tuna salad				$1.19	
10	pack	Twinkies (or other)				$3.50	
1	46 oz	V8 juice (or other)				$1.89	
1	gallon	Spring Water				$.59	
1	carton	Wheat thins				$2.00	

Appendix B: Safe Room Vent System

INSTALLING A SAFE ROOM HEPA FILTER SYSTEM

The safe room HEPA filter is designed to protect against biological agents and other unknown particulates.

Typical Safe Room Layout, Indicating Vent Locations

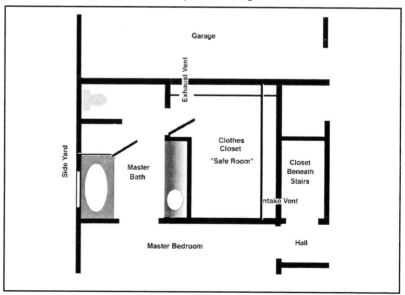

Below is a drawing of a typical installation, followed by a list of items for purchase at your local home improvement center, a list of tools you will need, and instructions on how to assemble the intake vent and exhaust vent. If you have money available, you may want to check the World Wide Web for manufacturers and installers of various emergency ventilation systems.

SHOPPING LIST

Purchase the following items from your local lumberyard, hardware store or home improvement center:

- 1—Roll 2" wide x 60 yard duct tape
- 1—1" x 3" x 6'-0" white wood board
- 1—2' x 4" x 8'-0
- One pound—Coated dry wall or sheet rock nails
- One pound,—6d nails, cement coated sinkers
- 1—Hunter 14 1/4" x 15 7/8" HEPA filter (about $70).
- 2–Metal 18" x 18" ventilator covers (flat)
- One tube—white acrylic latex caulk
- One tube—Liquid Nails general purpose cement
- Touch Up Paint—To match your existing wall color
- 1/4" x 5/8" self-sticking rubber weather stripping

Gather or purchase the following tools:

- Stud finder
- Carpenters square
- Tape measure
- 2 foot long level
- Spirit level (optional)
- Sheet rock saw, jig saw or saber saw
- Utility knife
- Cross cut saw (or power saw)
- Claw Hammer
- Paint brush
- Caulking gun

STEP-BY-STEP INSTRUCTIONS

1. Locate a place for the vent inlet in your proposed safe room. The

inlet vent should be on a wall that is common with the main part of the house. By drawing air from inside the house, instead of the outdoors, you reduce the risk of drawing in polluted air. If you tightly close all doors and windows at the first sign of an attack, and shut off any vent or air-conditioning fans prior to the time that any chemical or biological agents might reach your neighborhood, you have a much better chance of keeping the toxins outside your home. Most "fresh" air entering the house will seep through cracks under baseboards or seams around doors or windows. Since your home contains a considerable volume of air, and will be closed to the outdoors, you have a source of relatively clean air to draw in through your safe room ventilator. Some experts recommend that you shut off all air-conditioning if there are dangerous pollutants in the outside air, but if you are simply re-circulating inside air and you are not drawing air in from, or exhausting air out, this shouldn't be a concern. What's more, if you live in a hot climate, like Phoenix or Miami, you will need the air conditioner operating for as long as electricity is available. If possible, locate this intake vent toward the center of the safe room wall, and about a foot above the floor.

Safe Room Wall Cut away Showing HEPA Filter Installation

Bath Exhaust Fan

2"x4" studs on 16" centers

1'-2 1/2"

1'-2 1/2"

B

1'-4"

SAFE ROOM

1/2" Sheet Rock

Hunter HEPA filter, 14 1/4" x 15 7/8"

1/4" x 5/8" foam weather strip

1"x3"x14 1/2" white wood

18" x 18" Air intake grate

Air direction

1/2" Sheet Rock

A

120 volt Interior electrical cables

Wall end view   Wall cutaway as seen from Safe Room   Wall end view

Note: If there are any electrical outlets in the wall, on either side, you need to raise the bottom of the intake vent a few inches above the height of the outlet. Do not attempt to install the inlet vent within 16" of an electrical outlet.

2. Walk into the room on the opposite side of the wall where you plan to install your intake vent. Call this the "air supply room" because you will be drawing the air from this room. Gauge approximately where the intake vent will come through the wall. Make certain that there do not appear to be any obstructions where you plan to install your 18"x18" square vent cover on the wall, such as a fireplace, an electrical outlet, or another wall. If there is not sufficient room, you will have to relocate this vent. Use your deep wall stud detector to determine whether there are any electrical cables located beneath the selected spot.

Caution: Do not locate the vent within 16 inches of an electrical switch or outlet.

3. **Starting in the "air supply room,"** measure up 24 inches from the floor, and mark the spot on the wall. Lay your level across this mark and draw a 2-foot long horizontal line.

4. Using a stud finder, run it horizontally along the line. When you locate one of the vertical wooden studs that form the frame inside the wall, place marks above the edges of the stud. You can tell where the edges are because the indicator lights will flash on, and a laser line may appear on the wall above the edge of the stud. This stud will form the frame and support for one edge of your intake filter.

5. Move approximately 16 inches from the first stud and again run the stud finder along the level line to locate a second vertical stud. Mark the edge of the stud nearest the planned vent.

6. Measure the distance between the two closest marks, the marks that indicate the distance between the inside edges of the two studs. They should be about 14 1/2" apart. You are going to cut a rectangular piece of sheetrock from between these two studs; it will be about 14 1/2" wide by 16" high.

7. Make a horizontal cut between the studs. Use a screwdriver and hammer to tap a small hole through the wall on the line near one stud. Insert the point of your saw and cut along the horizontal line to the other stud.

8. By looking along the cut, locate the exact inside edge of each stud. Hold the level vertically over the edge and draw a 16" line up the inside or facing edge of each stud.

9. Hold the level sixteen inches above the bottom cut and draw a horizontal line between the studs.

10. Use your saw to cut out the remainder of this rectangle and set the piece of sheet rock aside. Make the two vertical cuts. Punch a hole at one remaining corner to insert the saw point, then make the final horizontal cut.

11. Measure the exact distance between the studs at both the top and bottom of the opening.

12. Install Pieces "A." Cut two pieces from the 2" x 4" x 8'-0" to fit snugly across these openings. They will be approximately 14 1/2" long.

13. Drive a nail a short way into the center of the flat side of each of the two pieces. These will serve as "handles" while you install them. You will be slipping one of them between the two layers of sheet rock at the top of the opening, so that it's bottom comes flush with the hole you've cut.

14. Cut the tip from the tube of Liquid Nails, insert it into the caulking gun, and squirt a little on each edge and both end of one of the pieces of 2" x 4" x 14 1/2". Carefully push this piece of 2"x4" into the opening at the top of the hole. When it appears flush with the edge of the sheet rock, check it with the spirit level to make certain that it is level.

15. Drive a sheet rock nail through the sheet rock into each end of the board, about two inches from the stud.

16. Squirt a little Liquid Nails on the edges and ends of the second piece of 2"x4" and insert it between the lower pieces of sheet rock. Make certain that you have a full 16" clearance between the inside

edges of the top and bottom 2"x4" boards.

17. Nail this 2"x4" in place through the dry wall. Let them set about 30 minutes for the cement to harden.

18. Pull the two nails that you used as handles from the 2"x4". Drive two more sheet rock nails, evenly spaced, into each edge of each horizontal 2x4.

19. Install Piece "B" (see diagram above). Cut four 14 1/2" long pieces from the 1"x43" x 8'-0" firing strip.

20. Squirt Liquid Nails on the flat side of one piece. Insert it into the opening, laying it on the lower piece with the cement against the new horizontal 2"x4". Position it so that its long narrow edge seats against the uncut sheetrock in the back of the opening. Using two 6 d sinker nails, fasten the ends of the 1" x 3" to the 2" x 4" below it.

21. Follow the same steps to install another 1" x 3" x1 4 1/2" pieces at the top of the opening.

22. Put the last two 1" x 3" x 14 1/2" pieces in on the sides of the opening, again, with their edges seated against the uncut sheet-rock in the back of the opening. The pieces should look like the diagram above. Let these pieces set for another half hour.

Note: The hole in the safe room side of the sheet rock will be a little smaller than the hole in the air supply room.

23. Use your thin screwdriver, or some other sharp item, for a punch. Place the point in one corner of the frame work, and drive it through the back layer of sheet rock. Repeat this step for each corner. When you return to the safe room, these four holes will mark the corners of the opening that you will be cutting in the sheet rock from that side.

24. Re-enter the Safe Room. Draw straight lines between the punched holes.

25. Use your saw to cut out this smaller piece of sheet rock.

26. Clean up the area with a vacuum cleaner.

27. Return to the Air Supply Room.

28. Cut four piece of 14 1/2" lengths from the 1/4" x 5/8" self-sticking rubber weather stripping and fasten them to the narrow facing edges of the 1"x3" boards you have installed. They form a flange against which you will seat the HEPA filter.

29. Unwrap and carefully insert your HEPA filter into the opening. It should press back firmly against the weather stripping. If it is too loose, apply some weather stripping around the edges of the opening to keep the filter from moving around. The edges must be tightly sealed. You must keep any air from going around the edges of the filter.

30. Still working from the air intake room, install the 18"x18" decorative grill over the filter. Hold it in position so that it looks about right. Put a couple of pencil marks on the wall. Use the level to make certain that you have it level. Screw it in place with the screws supplied.

31. You may elect not to put a grill over the hole on the inside of the safe room, but that is not advisable. You do not want anyone reaching through and touching what might be a toxic filter.

32. Use some spackle and your touch up paint to repair any scratches you may have made.

33. Congratulations! You have the intake filter installed. Tape a piece of plastic vapor barrier, or a couple of layers of trash bags, over the inside of the hole or the cover grate in the safe room so that air is not being passed through the filter until you are ready to use it. Should an emergency arise, remove the plastic so that air can pass through the filter.

THE EXHAUST VENT

The exhaust vent and fan are very important. By exhausting air from the upper part of the safe room. the fan will produce a vacuum that will draw air in to the safe room through the HEPA filter. The safe room air should be exhausted into a room that you are not likely to enter.

This fan should be located where you can easily access an existing electrical supply line. You will want to install a switch so that you can turn it on and off. You may purchase a low-volume, low-noise bathroom fan and necessary exhaust duct work from any home improvement center or hardware store. It will contain full installation instructions. Explain to the clerk that you are installing the fan by an existing electrical line, and he will provide the materials and instructions you require.

Buy a roll of duct tape and a sheet of polyethylene or other clear plastic sheeting, and keep them in the new safe room. If there is an biological or chemical attack within a few miles of your home, get your family into the safe room. Then, immediately tape the cracks around the door, and cover any ventilator or air-conditioning ducts by taping several layers of plastic trash bags over them. You cannot do this, however, unless you have a tank of compressed air or oxygen to enrich the air from time to time.

Warning: Oxygen is dangerous. You must not have an open flame or a source of electrical shock where you are using oxygen.

Appendix C: Items of Special Interest

COMMUNICATIONS EQUIPMENT

Cellular Phones

The rapidly expanding and changing cellular telephone market has made cell phones—feature for feature—almost commodities. It is not the cost of the phone that matters, but the carrier's calling areas and terms of contract that cause the prices and usefulness to vary. Check with knowledgeable associates and compare literature before making a choice.

Emergency radios

For reviews of various excellent emergency radios, along with prices, go to http://www.google.comand and enter "emergency radios."

Walkie Talkies

Motorola has been the leader in walkie talkies for many years, but because of advance in computers, communications, and miniaturization, there are some satisfactory competitive products available at lower prices. Again, go to http:/

/www.google.com and key in "walkie talkies." Among local retailers, check your own favorite locally owned stores as well as Radio Shack, Circuit City, Tweeters, Best Buys, Wal-mart, K-Mart, your warehouse clubs, and a host of others.

PROTECTIVE GEAR

Nuisance dust masks

While you may purchase nuisance dust masks at many local stores, the quality is often low. Many discount stores will sell you five nuisance masks for about $5, or a buck each. Since you can buy 50 3M brand SARs resistant surgical masks for only $19.95, a cost of only 40 cents each, why would you buy a mere nuisance dust mask.

Surgical masks (SARS resistant)

Although gas masks provide protection against chemical weapons, they are expensive, bulky, and their costly filters must be replaced over brief periods. Biological agents pose a considerably greater threat than chemical agents.

Biological infection is effectively prevented by using an appropriate filter that is tightly sealed around one's mouth and nose. Gas masks have the advantage of protecting the eyes from blood and other body wastes, but a pair of goggles worn above a high quality surgical mask can satisfy this need. Higher quality surgical masks successfully filter out particles greater than 0.5 microns. Anthrax spores are restricted by these fine filters. SARs is not.

The 3M website claims that its disposable High Filtra-tion Surgical Mask is a high quality surgical mask. The mask exceeds 99% filtration efficiency at only 0.1 micron. It features a comfortable soft ear loop design featuring a pad-ded nosepiece. They claim that the masks layers are bonded ultrasonically to eliminate sewing pinholes, which can allow bacteria to move across the mask.

You may increase the effectiveness of masks by using surgical tape to seal the edges of the mask to your face, creating a more reliable seal.

While most surgical masks filter particles 3-5 microns in size, the CDC believes that SARS is caused by the coronavirus, which is only 0.1 to 0.2 microns in size. Since this mask is 99% efficient at only 0.1 microns, it should generally be effective at stopping SARS.

This mask offers the advantage that it folds flat, unlike molded masks.

http://store.yahoo.com/safetyandsecuritycenter/hipeansuma.html offers them at 50 masks for $19.95.

Gas Masks and Protective Gear

I bought Israeli gas masks for my entire family for $10 to $15, including one filter each. The same mask is now advertised on various web sites at prices ranging from $38.95 to $144.95. Obviously, you need to shop around.

Many sites also advertise suits, safe room gear, etc. So, while most people seem quite disinterested in preparedness, it's obvious that many manufacturers, importers and distributors are making a lot of money by exploiting our fears.

Be prudent in deciding what you need, Don't allow yourself to be stampeded. Make your decisions, buy the products, learn to use them, and store them carefully where they will be available if and when you need them...just as you did with your kitchen fire extinguisher and home smoke detector.

HEPA Filters

FEMA recommends the use of a HEPA filter within the family safe room. I also recommend a second filter in the room through which you enter the safe room. Purchase a free standing HEPA filter at Sears, your home improvement center, and most discount chains.

Air Tanks

If you are unable to find a supply of clean safe air in tanks, consider investing in scuba gear. Take the training course. Then store the tanks and breathing apparatus in your safe room so that you can augment your air supply if you are, by some stretch of the imagination, threatened with chemical agents. (Your built-in HEPA filter system should handle biological toxins.)

DETECTORS

Smoke Detectors

Check your local home improvement center

Carbon Monoxide Detectors

Check your local home improvement center

Chemical and Biological Agent Detectors

Go to www.google.com or www.ask.com and key in either "chemical agent detectors" or "biological agent detectors" to view a list of suppliers and product reviews.

Scintillation Counters

Go to www.google.com or www.ask.com and key in "scintillation counter" to view a list of suppliers and product reviews.

SHELTER DESIGNS

There are scores of web sites offering shelter designs, but many of them are commercial sites and are profit oriented. The competence of the sponsors must be verified. There are also some very useful sites developed by interested and sometimes very knowledgeable people who offer advice and designs at no charge.

By comparing many designs, you will quickly begin to learn which designs and which sites are useful.

Go to http://www.fema.gov for free copies of shelter designs. Their work is thorough and excellent. Go to http://www.google.com and key in "Safe Room" or fallout shelter." A page will open listing manufacturers and suppliers of shelters and shelter components (such as doors & vent systems) and even free design packages.

FIRST AID

Surgical Gloves

To locate competitive prices on all manner of surgical supplies, go to http://www.google.comand key in the phrase, "surgical supplies."

First Aid Kits

Shop your local discount and warehouse stores.

Drugs, Medical Manuals, and Surgical Equipment

Consult your physician, and go to http://www.webmd.com.

Appendix D: Helpful Books & Movies

The books and motion pictures listed below are available through your local bookstore as well as on the Internet. Note that some on-line vendors offer used books at substantially discounted prices.

American Red Cross First Aid and Safety Handbook, by Kathleen A. Handal, Little Brown, 1992, $12.57.

"Every household should have a copy.", Frank Becker

Archer's and Bowhunter's Bible, by Lea Lawrence, Doubleday, 1993, $10.37.

Excerpt from page 54 "... than does a rucksack or fanny pack. In addition to hunting items-knife, game bags, and the... get lost or hurt, I'll survive comfortably. That knowledge means efficient back country hunting. The frame pack..."

The Encyclopedia of Edible Plants of North America, by Francois Couplan, James Duke (Foreword) (Paperback) McGraw-Hill, $19.95.

Excerpt from page 68 "... emollient. Pellitory must be used fresh, as it loses its medicinal properties on drying. The juice extracted from the plant has been employed for the same medicinal purposes as well. Pilea (G 4)... are one of the best wild vegetables. Their taste is exquisite, they can be gathered in..."

Empire of the Sun, 1987 (motion picture), Steven Spielberg; A young English boy struggles to survive under Japanese occupation during World War II.

Foxfire 11, by Kaye Carver Collins, Anchor, 1999, $15.95.

From the book's inside flap: "...in this age of technology and cyber-living, the books teach a philosophy of simplicity in living that is truly enduring in its appeal. This new volume--Foxfire 11-- celebrates the rituals and recipes of the Appalachian homeplace, including a one-hundred page section on herbal remedies, and segments about planting and growing a garden, preserving and pickling, smoking and salting, honey making, beekeeping, and fishing, as well as hundreds of the kind of spirited firsthand narrative accounts from Appalachian community members that exemplify the Foxfire style. Much more than "how-to" books, the Foxfire series is a publishing phenomenon and a way of life, teaching creative self-sufficiency, the art of natural remedies, home crafts, and other country folkways, fascinating to everyone interested in rediscovering the virtues of simple life."

Homeland Security Knowledge Base, http://www.twotiger-sonline.com/resources.html. Definitive website describing threats and much useful information.

Life After Terrorism: What you Need to Know to Survive in Today's World, by Bruce D. Clayton, Paladin Press, July, 2002, $21.95.

Synopsis from www.amazon.com. Protecting your family from terrorism in today's world requires an astonishing breadth of knowledge on topics ranging from microbiology and radiological defence to proper waste storage, government disaster response, and escape routes to and from where you live and work. In this book, Dr. Clayton takes a look at today's terrorist threats, assesses their dangers realistically, and explains in practical terms what you can do to reduce your risks. Hopefully your family will never be the victims of a terrorist attack, but after September, 11, do you want to bet on it? Where your loved one's lives are at stake, you can't afford to be naive or make mistakes. Besides, the information in this book is useful for other kinds of emergency, from a natural disaster to an outbreak of an infectious disease to domestic upheaval. The book will scare you, educate you, entertain you, and make you think. Most importantly, it will prepare you for life after terrorism.

Living Safe in an Unsafe World, by Kate Kelly, NAL Books, 2000, $14.95

From the cover: "*Living Safe in an Unsafe World* will provide you with all the up-to-date information you need to know to prepare for the unexpected, and will instill in you and your children a mind-set that will carry you through any creisis."

My Side of the Mountain, Jean Craighead George.

Amazon.com review: Every kid thinks about running away at one point or another; few get farther than the end of the block. Young Sam Gribley gets to the end of the block and keeps going--all the way to the Catskill Mountains of upstate New York. There he sets up house in a huge hollowed-out tree, with a falcon and a weasel for companions and his wits as his tool for survival. In a spellbinding, touching, funny account, Sam learns to live off the land, and grows up a little in the process. Blizzards, hunters, loneliness, and fear all battle to drive Sam back to city life. But his desire for freedom, independence, and adventure is stronger. No reader will be immune to the compulsion to go right out and start whittling fishhooks and befriending raccoons.

Red Dawn, John Milius, starring Patrick Swazey.

Plot Outline: It is the dawn of World War III. In mid-western America, a group of teenagers bands together to defend their town, and their country, from invading Soviet forces, surviving under deplorable conditions.

Simply Essential Disaster Preparation Kit, by Catherine Stuart, Self Counsel Press, 2003, $11.95.

From the back cover: ...designed to give individuals and families the information they need to prepare for, mitigate, and increase their chances of surviving a major disaster. The kit comes with tips on survival basics and checklists to help anyone prepare for disasters such as earthquakes, floods, tornadoes, ice storms, fire, and terrorist attacks. This essential kit includes the following information: - Assembling a disaster kit - Developing a family evacuation plan - Assembling a medical-supplies kit - Protecting your house and possessions.

Swiss Family Robinson, The, Johan Wyss.

"Shipwrecked! They must find a way to survive and trust in God to protect them on a wild island in the middle of nowhere." This text refers to an out of print or unavailable edition of this title. Some "dumbed down" contemporary editions provide a plot line, but very little of the essence and joy of the original.

U.S. Armed Forces Nuclear, Biological and Chemical Survival Manual, by Dick Couch, Basic Books, 2003, $14.95

From the Cover: "Experts agree that the next attack will not come in the same form as September 11. Every American faces the threat of nuclear, biological and chemical weapons. This handbook is your single most effective tool to protect yourself against the danger looming over our homeland."

U.S. Army Survival Manual, FM 21-76, Department of Defense, Apple Pie Publishers

Synopsis from http://www.amazon.com: If you want a manual that can help you in an emergency, deals with all manner of terrain, and is small enough to carry on all kinds of trips, this is the right one for you, $14.95.

Wild Medicinal Plants, by Anny Schneider, Stackpole Books, 2002, $20.37.

Book Description: A fully illustrated, full color guide to using some 80 wild medicinal plants found in North America. Includes descriptions and photographs of each plant species as well as information on where to find and how to use them. Matches a variety of illnesses with the plants that treat them, discusses how medicinal plants work and how and what parts of the plants should be gathered, and describes and illustrates toxic wild plants to avoid. Includes information for: Hawthorn, Adam's Flannel, Yarrow, Cinquefoil, Shepherd's Purse, Pussywillow, St. John's Wort, Huckleberry, Black Cherry, Bladderwrack, Watercress, Tansy, Barberry, Horseradish, Great Burdock, Curled Dock, Mallow, Stinging Nettle, Black Elder, Elecampane and 60 others. Includes scientific and common names for each plant.

Wilderness Living, by Gregory J. Davenport, Stackpole Books, 2001

Synopsis from www.amazon.com: Living by choice in the wild, not just surviving, can be a rewarding experience. This easy-to-use guide looks beyond the fundamentals of survival and examines the art of living long-term in the wilderness. Hunting techniques, meat preservation, clothing improvisations, water procurement, shelter design, and tool and basket-making are described in detail. Expert advice, straightforward text, and clear illustrations combine to make this book the authoritative text on primitive living, $16.95.

Wilderness Survival, by Gregory J. Davenport, Stackpole Books, 2001, $14.95.

Synopsis from www.amazon.comwww.amazon.com: During his intense training to become a US Air Force Survival Instructor, Gregory Davenport learned to adapt to adverse conditions and survive in every global climate. His experience and education are the foundation of this comprehensive, well organized, and user-friendly guide to staying alive in the wilderness. Using concise explanations and detailed illustrations, Davenport covers the five basic elements of survival providing the reader with complete information on how to stay calm and alive until the arrival of rescue.

Y2K Personal Survival Guide, Michael S. Hyatt, Regnery, 1999, $27.50

The Y2K Personal Survival Guide is a one-stop, comprehensive book that explains the ins-and-outs of Y2K preparation.

Index